# SOCRATES

**Vijay Tankha** studied at Delhi University and McGill University, Canada, where he did his Ph.D., specializing in Plato. He taught at St. Stephen's College, Delhi, for over three decades, retiring as Head, Department of Philosophy, in 2017. Over the years, he has written and published articles, both academic and popular, on philosophy and literature. He is the author of *Ancient Greek Philosophy* and *Poetry and Politics in Ancient Greece*. Two further books, one each on Plato and Aristotle, are forthcoming in this series.

CLASSICAL GREEK PHILOSOPHY

# SOCRATES

## The Barefoot Philosopher

Edited and Annotated by

Vijay Tankha

hachette INDIA

First published in paperback in 2026 by Hachette India
(Registered name: Hachette Book Publishing India Pvt. Ltd)
An Hachette UK company
www.hachetteindia.com

1



Graphics credit for the first and the last page of the book: Freepik.com. These pages have been designed using assets from www.freepik.com.



ISBN 978-93-5731-886-0

Hachette Book Publishing India Pvt. Ltd
4th & 5th Floors, Corporate Centre,
Plot No. 94, Sector 44, Gurugram 122003, India

Typeset in Garamond Baskerville BT 11.5/15
by InoSoft Systems, Noida

Printed and bound in India by
Manipal Technologies Limited

For Mahir

Barefoot and Beloved

# CONTENTS

# INTRODUCTION

Socrates is perhaps the best-known name in Western thought, if not in the whole world, rivalled only by the Buddha, Christ, or Confucius. All these men belonged to an oral tradition; what they thought and did was written down later. Socrates is known not through what he wrote but because others wrote down what he said. Despite our having no direct evidence of his ideas and beliefs, we have plenty of indirect evidence of both what he thought and what he did. We also have detailed information about his trial and execution and the reasons for it. He was the first philosopher, we are told, who was put to death. Aristotle, when a charge of impiety was brought against him later, left Athens, saying that he did not want the Athenians to sin against philosophy twice. Socrates was also in many ways the first philosopher of the western tradition and certainly its first public intellectual. His ideas were not clothed in arcane terminology or impenetrable mystery. There is nevertheless a cloak of uncertainty that clouds our vision of the man, not only because the diverse sources do not always agree in their details, but also because the most brilliant portrait of him is drawn at great length by his most illustrious student, Plato. It is really Plato who, occasionally stepping back, has given us as his surrogate, Socrates, the model thinker who made philosophy a 'way of life'. While other students and companions of Socrates produced dialogues in his memory (Aristotle calls them Socratic mimes), these works do not survive in their entirety, but their best-known authors are Antisthenes, Aeschines, Phaedo, and Eucleides. The only other reports that do, are in the writings of Xenophon and Aristophanes (the comic dramatist), from whose *Clouds*, Socrates descends, the very image of a hare-brained philosopher. A didactic teacher and conversationalist appears in several prose writings of Xenophon, an Athenian general who was Plato's contemporary. Together they offer very different pictures of Socrates. If we only had these, Socrates would not be a household name today. It is Plato who has conferred posthumous fame on his teacher. Not only is Socrates the principal speaker in almost all of Plato's dialogues, his most memorable images may well be Platonic creations.

The sum of these diverse depictions indicate just how well known Socrates must have been. The many lost Socratic dialogues of his acolytes are a testament to his unique personality, and its powerful effect on his times.

Reconciling or assessing these different versions has been an ongoing task for thinkers for the last two thousand years. Aristophanes's play is the earliest full fledged picture of Socrates, produced almost 25 years before his execution. Xenophon's memoirs, and Plato's dialogues were in all likelihood written sometime after Socrates's death. Though both knew him, Plato had a much closer association.

Xenophon (431–355 BCE) was a general, military historian, and author of several works on Socrates: *The Memoirs of Socrates (The Memorablia)*, *The Symposium*, *The Apology*, apart from other works on Greek history and a biography of the legendary Persian emperor, Cyrus. His version of Socrates is often dismissed as feeble compared to Plato's.

Plato (428–347BCE) is truly responsible for Socrates's fame. Without Plato's dialogues, Socrates might be no better known than Antisthenes or Aeschines, both of whom wrote Socratic dialogues. Socrates is a character in most of Plato's 30 odd dialogues. Though not entirely a creation, what Socrates says in them cannot be straightforwardly attributed to him; it is very hard to extract purely Socratic material from them. Yet glimpses of how Socrates argued, what he thought, may be inferred from what Plato writes. Thus the early Platonic dialogues are seen as a close representation of how Socrates conducted himself. Plato knew Socrates from his earliest years. His dialogues do give us glimpses of his personality. There is some point to isolating what may be typical Socratic elements in the Platonic dialogues. Thus we shall here bypass entirely what has been called the 'Socratic question', which scholars have inconclusively wrestled with: How Socratic/Platonic is Plato's Socrates?

There is a tradition that Socratic conversations and remarks were collector's items. The record of what he said (or might have) and to whom, formed the basis of the many dialogues that his followers composed. Diogenes, the third century BCE biographer, tells of one Simon the cobbler who would keep notes of what Socrates said on visits to his shop. The story seems unlikely since Socrates was famous for walking around barefoot, even in extreme cold. Yet it is indicative of how precious Socratic remarks were considered. In Plato's *Symposium*, one of the narrators, Apollodorus, says that he 'made it his care to know what Socrates says and does every day'. Having heard of the conversation from another associate, he cross-checked several points with Socrates himself. While it is true that Plato makes use of various distancing devices and narrative techniques to dramatically bring the Socratic past into the Platonic present, yet he also weaves in so many personal touches that we may be confident that they are not just figments of his imagination. Even if Xenophon was not present in some of the conversations that he records, he might have heard them from others, and noting them dramatically, as he does, would not for him have been unfaithful to the memory of Socrates. He writes at the opening of the *Memorablia*, that he will set down all that he can remember of Socrates's conversations. In his version of Socrates's trial he confirms that he got his information from one Hermogenes who was present there. Xenophon is being truthful, since it is known that he was away on an expedition at the time.

Plato and Xenophon, though contemporaries, do not acknowledge each other's writings. Xenophon mentions Plato once, Plato does not mention him at all. Nor do all representations of Socrates agree with each other. Xenophon's Socrates is very different from Plato's: perhaps there is as much of each in their separate portraits of him. The most glaring is in Aristophanes. In 423 BCE Aristophanes produced *The Clouds,* in which Socrates was a central character. What Socrates says and does in that play is at odds with what we know of him from other sources. We do not expect caricatures to mirror the person they depict. Yet for them to hit their mark, there must be some resemblance. Aristophanes made fun of other prominent persons in other plays, memorably the democratically elected ruler, Cleon. What he says of him seems rather stretched (his mother was a vegetable seller, he is illiterate, etc). The audience knew who Cleon was, the typical politician; not everything said about him had to be true. Cleon, in fact, sued the poet for defamation. Similarly, Socrates was very well known in Athens; *The Clouds* is not the only play that made fun of him, or of philosophers in general. The comic representations of Socrates, however they may distort, remain a testimony to his public image.

There is one further text, supposedly written shortly after the trial of Socrates (some think it formed the basis of the prosecution's speech). This was titled *The Indictment of Socrate*s by Polycrates, which possibly triggered the many defences that were written shortly thereafter, of which only Plato's and Xenophon's survive. Polycrates's work is lost and he is not mentioned directly by either Xenophon or Plato, but its key points, summarized by later writers, especially one Libanius who wrote an *Apologia Socratis* in 350 CE, can be inferred from what is said in his defence in the texts we quote. Polycrates, mentioned by other contemporaries of Socrates, was a thorough going democrat and the thrust of his charge was that Socrates hated the people (*misodemos*) and that his followers, especially Critias and Alcibiades, were corrupted by him. While no political charges were made against Socrates, it was his anti-democratic stance that most likely led to his indictment and trial. This does not mean that the charge of impiety and the worship of strange gods, though a screen for his accusers, was not a serious one: other thinkers had faced similar charges as well.

There were also other portraits of him in antiquity. While some of the details of his life as put together by later biographers like Diogenes in the third century BCE, may be apocryphal, there is an unbroken trail of reminiscence that leads from his presence in Athens in the middle of the fourth century BCE, even up to the present.

Since Diogenes used earlier works, as well as details familiar from Plato, his is a good starting point for a general life of Socrates, especially if his biography can be corroborated with what Xenophon and Plato tell us. There is a danger of circularity if, as some argue, Xenophon is often recapitulating Plato, while Plato is often thought to be creating rather than reporting Socrates. But Socrates is not a figment of their imagination, rather the source of their inspiration. Further, the comic representations of Socrates, even if distorted, remain a testimony to his public image — an anomaly, a distinct oddball, as philosophers or thinkers in general were perceived. Despite the different directions in which these representations pull, we have in the person of Socrates a philosopher who wrote nothing but left a lasting impression on the millennia that followed his barefoot steps.

NOTE: In what follows, I offer the reader selections from both Xenophon and Plato, which give us a picture of Socrates as well as some details of what he said and how he provoked the citizens of Athens. My own editorial introductions and comments on these passages are in italics to distinguish them from the selections I have made (translated from the Greek by a variety of scholars). Complete works of both Plato and Xenophon are easily available in both digital and print format.

# 1

# LIFE AND TIMES

## *Major Events. Wisdom as Ignorance. His Associates.*

***Socrates**, an Athenian citizen, fought for his city in a number of well-known battles during the early years of the Peloponnesian War which broke out in 432* BCE *and lasted 27 years. He was the subject of a play,* The Clouds, *by the comic poet Aristophanes, (produced when Socrates was 46) and was also caricatured by other writers of the time. At the end of the war in 404* BCE *with Athen's defeat, its democratic government was overthrown for a short period and ruled by a faction of the oligarchic party called the Thirty Tyrants. A few of these men were known associates of Socrates. Their rule was short and bloody. When the democrats overthrew them less than a year later, most were killed, including Plato's uncles, Critias and Charmides; others were exiled.*

*In the aftermath of this conflict, charges of impiety were brought against Socrates which may have been politically motivated. We may not be sure of the day or even the year of his birth, but he made 399 BCE famous by dying in it, having been found guilty by a democratic court. Accounts of his defence at his trial are recorded by both Plato and Xenophon.*

*A much longer account of Socrates's life and thought is found in Diogenes Laertius's* Lives of the Eminent Philosophers, *written in Greek around 230 BCE. Since Diogenes clearly used earlier lost works, as well as details familiar from Plato, his is a good starting point for a general life of Socrates. Diogenes writes:*

Socrates was the son of Sophroniscus, a statuary, and of Phaenarete, a midwife; as Plato records in his Theatetus, he was a citizen of Athens, of the borough of Alopece.

Having been a pupil of Anaxagoras… after the condemnation of Anaxagoras, he became a disciple of Archelaus, the natural philosopher. And, indeed, Aristoxenus says that he was very intimate with him.

For he was very clever in all rhetorical exercises, as Idomeneus also assures us. But the Thirty Tyrants forbade him to give lessons in the art of speaking and arguing, as Xenophon tells us. Aristophanes turns him into ridicule in his Comedies, as making the worse appear the better reason... He, likewise, was the first person who conversed about human life; and was also the first philosopher who was condemned to death and executed.

He then, perceiving that natural philosophy had no immediate bearing on our interests, began to enter upon moral speculations, both in his workshop and in the marketplace. And he said that the objects of his search were—

—Whatever good or harm can man befall in his own house.

And very often, while arguing and discussing points that arose, he was treated with great violence and beaten, and pulled about, and laughed at and ridiculed by the multitude. But he bore all this with great equanimity. So that once, when he had been kicked and buffeted about, and had borne it all patiently, and someone expressed his surprise, he said, 'Suppose an ass had kicked me, would you have had me bring an action against him?' And this is the account of Demetrius.

He had no need of travelling (though most philosophers did travel), except when he was bound to serve in the army. But all the rest of his life he remained in the same place, and in an argumentative spirit he used to dispute with all who would converse with him, not with the purpose of taking away their opinions from them, so much as of learning the truth, as far as he could do so, himself. And they say that Euripides gave him a small work of Heraclitus to read, and asked him afterwards what he thought of it, and he replied, 'What I have understood is good; and so, I think, what I have not understood is; only the book requires a Delian diver to get at the meaning of it.' He paid great attention also to the training of the body, and was always in excellent condition himself. Accordingly, he joined in the expedition to Amphipolis, and it was him who took up and saved Xenophon in the battle of Delium, when he had fallen from his horse; for when all the Athenians had fled, he retreated quietly, turning round slowly and watching to repel anyone who attacked him. He also joined in the expedition to Potidæa, which was undertaken by sea... And they say that on this occasion he remained the whole night in one place...

He was a man of great firmness of mind, and very much attached to the democracy, as was plain from his not submitting to Critias, when he ordered him to bring Leon of Salamis, a very rich man, before the Thirty, for the purpose of being murdered. And he alone voted for the acquittal of the ten generals; and when it was in his power to escape out of prison he would not do it; and he reproved those who bewailed his fate, and even while in prison, he delivered those beautiful discourses which we still possess.

He was a contented and venerable man. And once... when Alcibiades offered him a large piece of ground to build a house upon, he said, 'But if I wanted shoes, and you had given me a piece of leather to make myself shoes, I should be laughed at if I took it.' And often, when he beheld the multitude of things which were being sold, he would say to himself, 'How many things are there which I do not want.' And he was continually repeating these verses:

*For silver plate and purple useful are*
*For actors on the stage, but not for men.*

And he showed his scorn of Archelaus the Macedonian, and Scopas... and Eurylochus... (powerful tyrants), when he refused to accept their money, and to go and visit them. And he was so regular in his way of living, that it happened more than once when there was a plague at Athens, that he was the only person who did not catch it.

And he was a man able to look down upon any who mocked him. And he prided himself upon the simplicity of his way of life; and never exacted any pay from his pupils. And he used to say, that the man who ate with the greatest appetite, had the least need of delicacies; and that he who drank with the greatest appetite, was the least inclined to look for a draught which is not at hand; and that those who want fewest things are nearest to the Gods. And thus much, indeed, one may learn from the comic poets; who, without perceiving it, praise him in the very matters for which they ridicule him. Aristophanes speaks thus—

*Prudent man, who thus with justice long for mighty wisdom,*
*Happiness will be your lot in Athens, and all Greece too;*
*For you've a noble memory, and plenty of invention,*
*And patience dwells within your mind, and you are*

*never tired, Whether you're standing still or walking; and you care not for cold, Nor do you long for breakfast time, nor e'er give in to hunger; But wine and gluttony you shun, and all such kind of follies.*

...He used to praise leisure as the most valuable of possessions, as Xenophon tells us in his *Symposium*. And it was a saying of his that there was one only good, namely, knowledge; and one only evil, namely, ignorance; that riches and high birth had nothing estimable in them... And, moreover, he used to learn to play on the lyre when he had time, saying, that it was not absurd to learn anything that one did not know; and further, he used to dance frequently, thinking such an exercise good for the health of the body, as Xenophon relates.

He used also to say that the daimon foretold the future to him; and that to begin well was not a trifling thing, but yet not far from a trifling thing; and that he knew nothing, except the fact of his ignorance... Once, when he was asked what was the virtue of a young man, he said, 'To avoid excess in everything.' ...And when Euripides, in his *Auge* (a lost play), had spoken thus of virtue:

*'Tis best to leave these subjects undisturbed.*

...He rose up and left the theatre, saying that it was an absurdity to think it right to seek for a slave if one could not find him, but to let virtue be altogether disregarded. The question was once put to him by a man whether he would advise him to marry or not? And he replied, 'Whichever you do, you will repent it.'

And so he said to Aeschines, 'In three days I shall die.' And when he was about to drink the hemlock, Apollodorus presented him with a handsome robe, that he might expire in; and he said, 'Why was my own dress good enough to live in, and not good enough to die in?' ...It was a saying of his, too, 'That it is a good thing for a man to offer himself cheerfully to the attacks of the comic writers; for then, if they say anything worth hearing, one will be able to mend; and if they do not, then all they say is unimportant.'

And it was in consequence of such sayings and actions as these, that the priestess at Delphi was witness in his favour, when she gave Chaerephon this answer, which is so universally known—**Socrates of all mortals is the wisest.**

In consequence of the answer, he incurred great envy; and he brought envy also on himself by convicting men who gave themselves airs, of folly and ignorance... Plato in his *Apology*, say that these men brought the accusation—Anytus, and Lycon, and Meletus; Anytus, acting against him on behalf of the magistrates, and because of his political principles; Lycon, on behalf of the orators; and Meletus on behalf of the poets, all of whom Socrates used to pull to pieces...

But the sworn information, on which the trial proceeded, was drawn up in this fashion; for it is preserved to this day, says Phavorinus, in the temple of Cybele—Meletus, the son of Meletus, of Pithus, impeaches Socrates, the son of Sophroniscus, of Alopece. Socrates is guilty, inasmuch as he does not believe in the Gods whom the city worships, but introduces other strange deities. He is also guilty, inasmuch as he corrupts the young men, and the punishment he has incurred is death.

So when he had been condemned by 281 votes, being six more than were given in his favour, and when the judges were making an estimate of what punishment or fine should be inflicted on him, he said, 'My real opinion is, that as a return for what has been done by me, I deserve a maintenance in the Prytaneumn (*a central meeting place where state guests were entertained*) for the rest of my life.' So they condemned him to death, by 80 votes more than they had originally found him guilty. And he was put into prison, and a few days afterwards he drank the hemlock, having held many admirable conversations in the meantime, which Plato has recorded in the *Phædo*.

So he died; but the Athenians immediately repented of their action—they closed all the palaestrae and gymnasia, banished his accusers, and condemned Meletus to death; but they honoured Socrates with a brazen statue, which they erected in the place where the sacred vessels were kept.

He died in the first year of the 95th Olympiad, being 70 years of age. And this is the calculation of Demetrius Phalereus, for some say that he was but 60 years old when he died.

Of those who succeeded him, and who are called the Socratic school, the chiefs were Plato, Xenophon, and

Antisthenes. Of 'The Ten', as they are often called, the four most eminent were Aeschines, Phaedo, Euclides, and Aristippus. (Diogenes, *Lives,* 2.5.)

## Major Events in His Life

*Plato mentions three campaigns in which Socrates took part: the siege of Potidaea at the beginning of the Peloponnesian war, the battle of Amphipolis in 422* BCE, *and the defeat and subsequent retreat of the Athenians at Delium in Boeotia in 424* BCE. *Socrates served as a hoplite (a heavily armed foot soldier). Potidaea revolted from Athens and was defeated after a long siege. However, during the return, the Athenians were attacked and lost many men as well as their commanders. Socrates, then about 37, returned to Athens after about three years.It was during the expedition to Potidaea that Socrates saved Alcibiades's life and performed feats of endurance, which Alcibiades describes:*

He and I went on the expedition to Potidaea; there we messed together, and I had the opportunity of observing his extraordinary power of sustaining fatigue. His endurance was simply marvellous when, being cut off from our supplies, we were compelled to go without food—on such occasions, which often happen in the time of war, he was superior not only to me but to everybody; there was no one that compared to him. Yet at a festival he was the only person who had any real powers of enjoyment. Though not willing to drink, he could, if compelled, beat us all at that—wonderful to relate! No human being had ever seen

Socrates drunk. His fortitude in enduring cold was also surprising. There was a severe frost, for the winter in that region is really tremendous, and everybody else either remained indoors, or if they went out, they had on an amazing quantity of clothes, and were well shod, and had their feet swathed in felt and fleeces. In the midst of this, Socrates with his bare feet on the ice and in his ordinary dress marched better than the other soldiers who had shoes, and they shooted daggers at him because he seemed to despise them.

...I will also tell, if you please—and indeed I am bound to tell—of his courage in battle; for who but he saved my life? Now this was the engagement in which I received the prize of valour: I was wounded and he would not leave me, but he rescued me and my arms. He ought to have received the prize of valour which the generals wanted to confer on me partly on account of my rank, and I told them so (this, again, Socrates will not deny). But he was more eager than the generals that I and not he should have the prize (Plato, *Symposium*, 220d–e.)

*The battle of Delium was another Athenian disaster where again they lost their commanders. Alcibiades reports Socrates's conduct during the retreat*:

There was another occasion on which his behaviour was very remarkable—in the flight of the army after the battle of Delium, where he served among the heavy-armed. I had a better opportunity of seeing him than at Potidaea, for I myself was on horseback and therefore comparatively out of danger. He and Laches were retreating, for the troops were in flight, and I met them and told them not to be discouraged and promised to remain with them; and there you might see him... just as he is in the streets of Athens, stalking like a pelican, and rolling his eyes, calmly contemplating enemies as well as friends, and making very intelligible remarks to anybody, even from a distance, that whoever attacked him would be likely to meet with a stout resistance. And in this way, he and his companion escaped—for this is the sort of man who is never touched in war; those only are pursued who are running away headlong. I particularly observed how superior he was to Laches in presence of mind (Plato, *Symposium*, 221a.)

*Laches, a general, after whom Plato names a dialogue that discusses courage, speaks of Socrates during the retreat*:

*Laches*: Indeed, Lysimachus, he is a person you must not lose hold of; for I have observed him elsewhere too keeping up not merely his father's but his country's name. He accompanied me in the retreat from Delium and I assure you that if the rest had chosen to be like him, our city would be holding up her head and would not then have had such a terrible fall. (Plato, *Laches,* 181a-b.)

*We next hear of him in the public eye in 406 BCE when after the naval victory at Arginusae six generals who commanded the fleet were summarily tried and executed for not picking up the dead and injured, but pursuing the enemy instead. Socrates narrates this incident in Plato's* Apology.

*Socrates*: I, men of Athens, never held any other office in the state, but I was a pyrtanes (*one of 50 chosen by lot to sit on the Council)*; and it happened that my tribe held the presidency when you wished to judge collectively, not severally, the ten generals who had failed to gather up the slain after the naval battle; this was illegal, as you all agreed afterwards. At that time I was the only one of the *prytaneis* who opposed doing anything contrary to the laws, and although the orators were ready to impeach and arrest me, and though you urged them with shouts to do so, I thought I must run the risk to the end with law and justice on my side, rather than join with you when your wishes were unjust, through fear of imprisonment or death. (Plato, *Apology*, 31c.)

*Two years later with equal courage, he resisted an order given by the newly established oligarchy of the Thirty. These men were responsible for a series of judicial murders, especially of wealthy citizens whose property they coveted. The incident occurred after the end of the Peloponnesian War and about five years before his trial.*

*Socrates*: After the oligarchy was established, the Thirty sent for me with four others to come to the rotunda (*circular building used by council*) and ordered us to bring Leon from Salamis to be put to death. They gave many such orders to others also, because they wished to implicate as many in their crimes as they could. Then I, however, showed again, by action, not in word only, that I did not care a whit for death if that be not too rude an expression, but that I did care with all my might not to do anything unjust or unholy. For that government, with all its power, did not frighten me into doing anything unjust, but when we came out of the rotunda, the other four went to Salamis and arrested Leon, but I simply went home; and perhaps I should have been put to death for it, if the government had not quickly been put down. Of these facts you can have many witnesses. (Plato, *Apology*, 32c.)

*He was saved from the consequences of his action by the counter-revolution which restored the democracy a short time later. It was under a democratic government that he was condemned and put to death. Plato writes of this in the seventh Letter:*

But by some mischance, some of those in power brought my friend Socrates to trial on an infamous charge, the last that should ever have been brought against him. It was impiety that some of them accused him of, and the others condemned him and put him to death — the very man who had refused to have any hand in arresting one of their own friends when they themselves were in exile and misfortune. (Plato, *Letter*. 7, 325b–c.)

## Socrates's Wisdom

*The most memorable detail about Socrates is his claim to know only that he knew nothing. Over the ages Socratic ignorance became a mark of philosophical wisdom. It has been variously interpreted and understood. In Plato's works, Socratic ignorance is limited to questions about the nature of virtue. He is not for instance, marked as a sceptic about knowledge, even if he is sometimes agnostic about the after life. In Plato's account of his trial the oracle said 'no man is wiser than Socrates.' This is more in keeping with the celebrated ambiguity of the oracle, which did not positively declare Socrates to be wise, rather, it put limits on the wisdom of others (no one is wiser than him). In Xenophon's version the oracle marks him out not as the wisest, but as the most ethical of men.*

*Socrates*: Once on a time when Chaerephon made inquiry at the Delphic oracle concerning me, in the presence of many people, Apollo answered that no man was more free than I, or more just, or more prudent. (Xenophon, *Apology*, 13)

*Socrates*: The fact is, men of Athens, that I have acquired this reputation on account of nothing else than a sort of wisdom. What kind of wisdom is this? Just that which is perhaps human wisdom. For perhaps I really am wise in this wisdom... For the word which I speak is not mine... For of my wisdom — if it is wisdom at all — and of its nature, I will offer you the god of

Delphi (Apollo) as a witness. You know Chaerephon... He was my comrade from a youth and the comrade of your democratic party, and shared in the recent exile and came back with you. And you know the kind of man Chaerephon was, how impetuous in whatever he undertook. Well, once he went to Delphi and made so bold as to ask the oracle this question; he asked if there were anyone wiser than I. Now the Pythia (Apollo's priestess) replied that there was no one wiser. And about these things his brother here will bear you witness, since Chaerephon is dead... For when I heard this, I thought to myself: What in the world does the god mean, and what riddle is he propounding? For I am conscious that I am not wise either much or little. What then does he mean by declaring that I am the wisest? He certainly cannot be lying, for that is not possible for him. And for a long time I was at a loss as to what he meant; then with great reluctance I proceeded to investigate him somewhat as follows.

I went to one of those who had a reputation for wisdom thinking that there, if anywhere, I should prove the utterance wrong and should show the oracle This man is wiser than I, but you said I was wisest. So examining this man — it was one of the public men with regard to whom I had this kind of experience, and conversing with him, this man seemed to me to seem to be wise to many other people and especially to himself, but not to be so; and then I tried to show him that he thought he was wise, but was not. As a result, I became hateful to him and to many of those present. And so, as I went away, I thought to myself, I am wiser than this man; for neither of us really knows anything fine and good, but this man thinks he knows something when he does not, whereas I, as I do not know anything, do not think I do either. I seem, then, in just this little thing to be wiser than this man at any rate, that what I do not know I do not think I know either. (Plato, *Apology*, 20d–21d.)

## His Marriage

*Socrates was married to Xanthippe, and had three sons, the youngest was an infant when Socrates was executed. In an anecdote related by Xenophon, Socrates, and his friends are being entertained with music and some gymnastic spectacles, Socrates shares a remark about the nature of women, not very different from what Plato says about them in the Republic.*

*Socrates*: I see that the dancing girl here is standing ready, and that some one is bringing her some hoops.

At that, the other girl began to accompany the dancer on the flute, and a boy at her elbow handed her up the hoops until he had given her 12. She took these, and as she danced she kept throwing them whirling into the air, observing the proper height to throw them so as to catch them in a regular rhythm.

As Socrates looked on he remarked: This girl's feat, gentlemen, is only one of many proofs that woman's nature is really not a whit inferior to man's except in its lack of judgment and physical strength. So if any one of you has a wife, let him confidently set about teaching her whatever he would like to have her know.

If that is your view, Socrates, asked Antisthenes, how does it come that you don't practise what you preach by yourself educating Xanthippe, but live with a wife who is the hardest to get along with of all the women there are, yes, or all that ever were, I suspect, or ever will be?

— Because, he replied, I observe that men who wish to become expert horsemen do not get the most docile horses but rather those that are high-mettled, believing that if they can manage this kind, they will easily handle any other. My course is similar. Mankind at large is what I wish to deal and associate with; and so I have got her, well assured that if I can endure her, I shall have no difficulty in my relations with all the rest of human kind.' (Xenophon, *Symposium*, 2.7–10.)

## His Associates

*Both Plato and Xenophon name various persons who spent time with Socrates. Some wrote Socratic dialogues, only fragments of which remain. Chaerephon, whom Plato describes as 'a little mad' went to the oracle at Delphi. Aristophanes makes fun of him in* The Clouds *and in* The Birds, *describes him as a Spartan-lover, hungry and unwashed. Socrates's most celebrated associate, however, was Alcibiades a wealthy young noble whose whirlwind political life is the subject of many accounts. Alcibiades makes a memorable entrance in Plato's Symposium and at least one Platonic dialogue bears his name. Famously infamous in his own times, his anti-democratic activities were cited as a reason for Socrates's indictment. Entire books have been written about him and he figures as a major player in Thucydides's* History of the Peloponnesian War. *In their portraits of him, both Xenophon and Plato try to show that Socrates could not be held responsible for his actions.*

***Alcibiades***

Among the associates of Socrates were Critias and Alcibiades; and none wrought so many evils to the state. For Critias in the days of the oligarchy bore the palm for greed and violence. Alcibiades, for his part, exceeded all in licentiousness and insolence under the democracy. Now I have no intention of excusing the wrong these two men wrought the state but I will explain how they came to be with Socrates. Ambition was the very life-blood of both: No Athenian was ever like them. They were eager to get control of everything and to outstrip every rival in notoriety. They knew that Socrates was living on very little and yet was wholly independent; that he was strictly moderate in all his pleasures; and that in argument he could do what he liked with any Disputant ... I believe that, had heaven granted them the choice between the life they saw Socrates leading and death, they would have chosen rather to die. Their conduct betrayed their purpose, for as soon as they thought themselves superior to their fellow-disciples they sprang away from Socrates and took to politics. It was for political ends that they had wanted Socrates... So long as they were with Socrates, they found in him an ally who gave them strength to conquer their evil passions. But when they parted from him, Critias fled to Thessaly, and got among men who put lawlessness before justice. While Alcibiades, on account of his beauty, was hunted by many great ladies, and because of his influence at Athens and among her allies he was spoilt by many powerful men. And as athletes who gain an easy victory in the games are apt to neglect their training, so the honour in which he was held, the cheap triumph he won with the people, led him to neglect himself. Such was their fortune: And when to pride of birth, confidence in wealth, vainglory, and much yielding to temptation were added corruption and long separation from Socrates, what wonder if they grew overbearing? (Xenophon, *Memorabilia*, 1.2.12–26.)

*A fragment from Antisthenes records Socrates admitting his love for Alcibiades.*

*Socrates*: If I thought I knew some art by which I could do good to men, I should have charged myself with great folly: But, as it is, I thought that these things came to me as a divine gift for the sake of Alcibiades. And there is nothing that calls for surprise in that. Through the love which I felt for Alcibiades I had had the same experience as the Bacchae. For the Bacchae, when they are inspired, draw up milk and honey from the wells from which other people cannot even get water. And so I too, though I have no science with which I could help a man by instructing him in it, nevertheless felt that by being with him I could make him better through my love for him. (Oxyrhynchus, *Papyri*, Part xiii.)

***Charmides***

*One of the noble-born youths who spent time with Socrates, Charmides became notorious for his role in the oligarchic overthrow of the democracy. Plato wrote a dialogue named after him in which Socrates discusses self-control and self-knowledge, with him as a young lad, traits he lacked when he was older. This selection from Xenophon, shows Socrates's attitude to democracy, denigrating the mass of citizens as fools.*

When he observed that Charmides, Glaucon's son, was reluctant to speak in the Assembly or to take part in politics despite being a remarkable man and more capable than contemporary politicians, he said:

*Socrates*: Tell me, Charmides, if someone were good enough to win the garland at our most prestigious competitions, and so bring honor upon himself and enhance the reputation of his native land throughout Greece, but refused to compete, what kind of man would you consider him to be?

— Clearly a poltroon and a coward, he said.

*Socrates*: Then if a man were to shrink from state business though capable of discharging it with advantage to the state and honour to himself, wouldn't it be reasonable to think him a coward?

— Perhaps; but why ask me that?

— Because I fancy that you shrink from work that is within your powers, work in which it is your duty as a citizen to take a hand.

— What makes you think so? In what sort of work have you discovered my powers?

— In your intercourse with public men. Whenever they take counsel with you, I find that you give excellent advice, and whenever they make a mistake, your criticism is sound.

— A private conversation is a very different thing from a crowded debate, Socrates.

— But, you know, a man who is good at figures counts as well in a crowd as in solitude; and those who play the harp best in private excel no less in a crowd.

— But surely you see that bashfulness and timidity come natural to a man, and affect him far more powerfully in the presence of a multitude than in private society?

— Yes, and I mean to give you a lesson. The wisest do not make you bashful, and the strongest do not make you timid; yet you are ashamed to address an audience of mere dunces and weaklings. Who are they that make you ashamed? For these are the people who make up the Assembly. You behave like a man who can beat trained athletes and is afraid of amateurs! You are at your ease when you talk with the first men in the state, some of whom despise you, and you are a far better talker than the ordinary run of politicians; and yet you are shy of addressing men who never gave a thought to public affairs and haven't learnt to despise you, all because you fear ridicule!

— Well, don't you think the Assembly often laughs at sound argument?

— Yes, and so do the others; and that's why I am surprised that you, who find it easy to manage them when they do it, think you will be quite unable to deal with the Assembly. My good man, don't be ignorant of yourself: Don't fall into the common error. For so many are in such a hurry to pry into other people's business that they never turn aside themselves. Don't refuse to face this duty then: Strive more earnestly to pay heed to yourself; and don't neglect public affairs, if you have the power to improve them. (Xenophon, *Memorabilia*, 3.7.1–9.)

### *Aristippus*

Aristippus was born in Cyrene, but went to Athens, drawn by the fame of Socrates. He played the sophist, as Phanias the Peripatetic says, he was the first of the Socratics to charge fees and send money to his teacher. He once sent Socrates 20 minae (*a very large sum*) but found them quickly sent back. Socrates said that his daimonion (*his spirit-guide*) would not let him keep the money; he was disgusted with Aristippus for sending it. (Diogenes Laertius, *Lives*, 2.65.)

### *Aspasia*

*Aspasia lived with the famous Athenian statesman Pericles as his mistress for about 20 years. Much reviled in Comedy, she was routinely blamed for starting the war with Sparta. In Plato's Menexenus, a response to Pericles's famous Funeral Oration, she is cast as the one who really composed his speech. Socrates, ironically, attributes his oratorical skill to her. Plutarch (46–120* CE*) probably from his reading of Plato, narrates the story that Socrates visited her.*

They say that Aspasia, emulated Thargelia, an Ionian woman from a previous age, by targeting the most powerful men. This Thargelia, with an attractive appearance and charm combined with cleverness, bedded a large number of Greek men, and brought all those who associated with her over to the King, sowing the seeds of Medism (Persian manners) in their cities through them because of their power and importance. Some say that Pericles's enthusiasm for Aspasia was because of her wisdom and political expertise. Witness the fact that sometimes Socrates used to visit her, with his associates, and his companions brought their wives to her, even though the business she presided over wasn't decent, or respectable — grooming young girls as prostitutes. Aeschines the Socratic says that Lysicles the sheep dealer, too, from being a person of low birth and humble talents became first among the Athenians through his association with Aspasia after the death of Pericles. (Plutarch, *Life of Pericles*, 24.3–6.)

*Menexenus*: You are always deriding the orators, Socrates. And truly I think that this time the selected speaker will not be too well-prepared; for the selection is being made without warning, so that the speaker will probably be driven to improvise his speech.

*Socrates*: Why so, my good sir? Each one of these men has speeches readymade; and what is more, it is in no wise difficult to improvise such things. For if it were a question of eulogizing Athenians before an audience of Peloponnesians, or Peloponnesians before Athenians, there would indeed be need of a good orator to win credence and credit; but when a man makes his effort in the presence of the very men whom he is praising, it is no difficult matter to win credit as a fine speaker.

...

*Meno*: And do you think that you yourself would be able to make the speech, if required and if the Council were to select you?

*Soc*: That I should be able to make the speech would be nothing wonderful, Menexenus; for she who is my instructor is by no means weak in the art of rhetoric; on the contrary, she has turned out many fine orators, and amongst them one who surpassed all other Greeks, Pericles, the son of Xanthippus.

*Meno*: Who is she? But you mean Aspasia, no doubt.

*Soc*: I do and also Connus the son of Metrobius; for these are my two instructors, the one in music, the other in rhetoric. So it is not surprising that a man who is trained like me should be clever at speaking... (and) win credit by praising Athenians before an Athenian audience.(Plato, *Menexenus*, 236a.)

# 2

# IMAGES OF THE MAN

## *Procurer. Gadfly. Midwife. In the Clouds.*

*Socrates's remarkable appearance and unusual behaviour was of considerable interest to his contemporaries. Descriptions as well as caricatures were as much a part of his legend as what he said and did. There are a variety of reports. His eyes were prominent, his nose upturned, lips thick, and his belly large — features customarily attributed by the Athenians to satyrs and silenoi. Satyrs are sometimes depicted on vases as having a very high hairline, which may be why Socrates was thought to be bald. He was known to walk barefoot.*

Ameipsias (*a comic playwright, and contemporary of Aristophanes, in his* Konnos), introduces him on the stage in a cloak, and speaks thus of him:

O Socrates, among few men the best,
And among many vainest; here at last
You come to us courageously — but where,
Where did you get that cloak? So strange a garment,
Some leather cutter must have given you
By way of joke: and yet this worthy man,
Though ne'er so hungry, never flatters anyone.

Aristophanes too, exposes his contemptuous and arrogant disposition, speaking thus:

— You strut along the streets, and look around you proudly,
And barefoot many ills endure, and hold your head above us. (D.L.2.28)

*Occasions when he does wear sandals are so rare as to be worthy of note. Apollodorus, recalls his meeting Socrates en route to a party, in Plato's Symposium:*

That he met Socrates fresh from the bath and sandalled; and as the sight of the sandals was unusual, he asked him whither he was going that he had been converted into such a beau:

To a banquet at Agathon's, he replied, whose invitation to his sacrifice of victory I refused yesterday, fearing a crowd, but promising that I would come today instead; and so I have put on my finery, because he is such a fine man. (Plato, *Symposium*, 174a.)

## His Ugliness

The wealthy Callias is greatly enamoured of the young and beautiful Critobulus. A mock beauty-contest between him and Socrates involves a detailed description of himself by the philosopher. Critobulus gets into trouble by his definition of beauty. In the ensuing discussion both disputants use only one word, Kalos, which means not only beautiful or handsome but also glorious, noble, excellent; starting with the first meaning, it soon shifts to the last.

*Callias*: Critobulus, are you going to refuse to enter the lists in the beauty contest with Socrates?

— Undoubtedly, said Socrates, for probably he notices that the procurer stands high in the favour of the judges.

— But yet in spite of that, retorted Critobulus, I do not shun the contest. So make your plea, if you can produce any profound reason, and prove that you are more handsome (kalos) than I. Only, let some one bring the light close to him.

— The first step, then, in my suit, said Socrates, is to summon you to the preliminary hearing; be so kind as to answer my questions.

— And you proceed to put them.

— Do you hold, then, that beauty is to be found only in man, or is it also in other objects?

*Crt.*: In faith, my opinion is that beauty is to be found quite as well in a horse or an ox or in any number of inanimate things. I know, at any rate, that a shield may be beautiful, or a sword, or a spear.

*Soc*: How can it be that all these things are beautiful when they are entirely dissimilar?

— Why, they are beautiful and fine answered Critobulus, if they are well-made for the respective functions for which we obtain them, or if they are naturally well-constituted to serve our needs.

*Soc*: Do you know the reason why we need eyes?

*Crt.*: Obviously to see with.

— In that case, it would appear without further ado that my eyes are finer ones than yours.

— How so?

— Because, while yours see only straight ahead, mine, by bulging out as they do, see also to the sides.

*Crt.*: Do you mean to say that a crab is better equipped visually than any other creature?

*Soc*: Absolutely; for its eyes are also better set to insure strength.

*Crt.*: Well, let that pass; but whose nose is finer (handsome), yours or mine?

*Soc*: Mine, I consider, granting that Providence made us noses to smell with. For your nostrils look down toward the ground, but mine are wide open and turned outward so that I can catch scents from all about.

*Crt.*: But how do you make a snub nose handsomer than a straight one?

*Soc*: For the reason that it does not put a barricade between the eyes but allows them unobstructed vision of whatever they desire to see: Whereas a high nose, as if in despite, has walled the eyes off one from the other.

— As for the mouth, said Critobulus, I concede that point. For if it is created for the purpose of biting off food, you could bite off a far bigger mouthful than I could. And don't you think that your kiss is also the more tender because you have thick lips?

*Soc*: According to your argument, it would seem that I have a mouth more ugly even than an ass's. But do you not reckon it a proof of my superior beauty that the River Nymphs, goddesses as they are, bear as their offspring the Silenoi (*followers of Dionysus, wise, but given to debauchery and drunkeness*), who resemble me more closely than they do you?

— I cannot argue any longer with you, answered Critobulus.

*Soc*: let them distribute the ballots, so that I may know without suspense what fine or punishment I must undergo. Only let the balloting be secret, for I am afraid that the wealth you and Antisthenes possess will overmaster me.

So the maiden and the lad turned in the ballots secretly. While this was going on, Socrates saw to it that the light should be brought in front of Critobulus, so that the judges might not be misled, and stipulated that the prize given by the judges to crown the victor should be kisses and not ribbons. When the ballots were turned out of the urn and proved to be a unanimous verdict in favour of Critobulus — Faugh! exclaimed Socrates; your money, Critobulus, does not appear to resemble Callias's. For his makes people more honest, while yours is about the most potent to corrupt men, whether members of a jury or judges of a contest.

(Xenophon, *Symposium*, 5.1–6.1.)

## Procurer (Pimp)

*There are other even more salubrious images of Socrates, which he himself endorses, even as he elevates their meaning. Along with Antisthenes (also wrote Socratic dialogues), Socrates is in conversation with the wealthy Callias and others. Socrates has just described himself as a procurer.*

*Callias*: And now, Socrates, what can you advance in support of your pride in that disreputable profession that you mentioned?

*Socrates*: Let us first come to an understanding on the functions that belong to the procurer. Do not hesitate to answer all the questions I ask you, so that we may know our points of agreement. Is that your pleasure?

— Certainly, was their reply; and when they had once started with 'certainly', that was the answer they all made to his questions thereafter.

*Soc*: Well, then, you consider it the function of a good procurer to render the man or the woman whom he is serving attractive to his or her associates?

*All*: Certainly.

*Soc*: Now, one thing that contributes to rendering a person attractive is a comely arrangement of hair and clothing, is it not?

*All*: Certainly.

*Soc*: This, also, we know, do we not, that it is in a man's power to use the one pair of eyes to express both friendship and hostility?

— Certainly.

— And again, it is possible to speak both modestly and boldly with the same voice?

— Certainly.

— Moreover, are there not words that create ill feeling and others that conduce to friendliness?

— Certainly.

— Now the good procurer would teach only the words that tend to make one attractive, would he not?

— Certainly.

— Which one would be the better? The one who could make people attractive to a single person or the one who could make them attractive to many?

...

Remarking that they were all of one mind on this point as on the others, he went on:

— If a person could render people attractive to the entire community, would he not satisfy the requirements of the ideal procurer?

— Indubitably.

— And so, if one could produce men of this type out of his clients, he would be entitled to feel proud of his profession and to receive a high remuneration, would he not?

All agreeing on this point, too, he added: Antisthenes here, seems to me to be a man of just that sort.

Antisthenes asked: Are you resigning your profession to me, Socrates?

— Assuredly, for I see that you have brought to a high state of perfection the complementary trade.

— What is that?

— The profession of go-between.

Antisthenes was much incensed and asked: What knowledge can you possibly have of my being guilty of such a thing as that?

*Soc*: I know several instances, I know that you acted the part between Callias here and the scholar Prodicus, when you saw that Callias was in love with philosophy and that Prodicus wanted money. I know also that you did the same for Hippias, the Elean, from whom Callias got his memory system; and as a result, Callias has become more amorous than ever, because he finds it impossible to forget any beauty he sees. And just recently, you remember, you introduced the stranger from Heraclea to me. For this I am indeed grateful to you; for I look upon him as endowed with a truly noble nature… It is the witnessing of your talent at achieving such a result that makes me judge you an excellent go-between. For the man who can recognize those who are fitted to be mutually helpful and can make them desire one another's acquaintance, that man, in my opinion, could also create friendship between cities and arrange suitable marriages, and would be a very valuable acquisition as friend or ally for both states and individuals. But you got indignant, as if you had received an affront. (ibid. 4. 54–58, 5. 58–61)

## Gadfly or Sting-Ray

*Socrates at his trial reminds the jury of the important function that he performs in keeping the city on its toes. More specifically his questions sting those whom he interacts with,*

*Socrates*: And so, men of Athens, I am now making my defence not for my own sake, as one might imagine, but far more for yours, that you may not by condemning me err in your treatment of the gift the God gave you. For if you put me to death, you will not easily find another, who, to use a rather absurd figure, attaches himself to the city as a gadfly to a horse which, though large and well-bred, is sluggish on account of his size and needs to be aroused by stinging. I think the god fastened me upon the city in some such capacity, and I go about arousing, and urging and reproaching each one of you, constantly alighting upon you everywhere the whole day long. Such another is not likely to come to you, gentlemen. (Plato, *Apology*, 30e.)

*In Plato's* Meno, *Socrates has the effect of a sting-ray on those he interacts with.*

*Meno*: Socrates, I used to be told, before I began to meet you, that yours was just a case of being in doubt yourself and making others doubt also. And so now I find you are merely bewitching me with your spells and incantations, which have reduced me to utter perplexity. And if I am indeed to have my jest, I consider that both in your appearance and in other respects you are extremely like the flat torpedo sea-fish; for it benumbs anyone who approaches and touches it, and something of the sort is what I find you have done to me now. For in truth, I feel my soul and my tongue quite benumbed, and I am at a loss what answer to give you. And yet on countless occasions I have made abundant speeches to various people and very good speeches they were, so I thought — but now I cannot say one word as to what it is.

You are well-advised, I consider, in not voyaging or taking a trip away from home; for if you went on like this as a stranger in any other city you would very likely be taken up for a wizard.(Plato, *Meno*, 80a.)

## Like a Satyr

*Although he looks like a satyr (known for their lasciviousness), his outward appearance is deceptive. His speech is more potent than Marsyas (who dared to compete with Apollo). Alcibiades, rather drunk, speaks in praise of Socrates in Plato's Symposium.*

*Alcibiades*: I shall praise Socrates in a figure which will appear to him to be a caricature, and yet I speak, not to make fun of him, but only for the truth's sake. I say, that he is exactly like the busts of Silenus, which are set up in the statuaries' shops, holding pipes and flutes in their mouths; and they are made to open in the middle, and have images of gods inside them. I say also that he is like Marsyas the satyr. You yourself will not deny, Socrates, that your face is like that of a satyr. Aye, and there is a resemblance in other points too. For example, you are a bully, as I can prove by witnesses, if you will not confess. And are you not a flute-player? That you are, and a performer far more wonderful than Marsyas. He indeed with instruments used to charm the souls of men by the power of his breath... But you produce the same effect with your words only, and do not require the flute: That is the difference between you and him. When we hear any other speaker, even a very good one, he produces absolutely no effect upon us, or not much, whereas the mere fragments of you and your words, even at second hand, and however imperfectly repeated, amaze and possess the souls of every man, woman, and child who comes within hearing of them. And if I were not afraid that you would think me hopelessly drunk, I would have sworn as well as spoken to the influence which they have always had and still have over me. For my heart leaps within me more than that of any Corybantes, (*Corybantic revellers participated through frenzied dancing in rites celebrating the goddess Cybele*) and my eyes rain tears when I hear them. And I observe that many others are affected in the same manner. I have heard Pericles and other great orators, and I thought that they spoke well, but I never had any similar feeling; my soul was not stirred by them, nor was I angry at the thought of my own slavish state.

But this Marsyas has often brought me to such a pass, that I have felt as if I could hardly endure the life which I am leading; and I am conscious that if

I did not shut my ears against him, and fly as from the voice of the siren, my fate would be like that of others — he would transfix me, and I should grow old sitting at his feet. For he makes me confess that I ought not to live as I do, neglecting the wants of my own soul, and busying myself with the concerns of the Athenians; therefore I hold my ears and tear myself away from him. And he is the only person who ever made me ashamed, which you might think not to be in my nature, and there is no one else who does the same. For I know that I cannot answer him or say that I ought not to do as he bids, but when I leave his presence the love of popularity gets the better of me. And therefore I run away and fly from him, and when I see him I am ashamed of what I have confessed to him. Many a time have I wished that he were dead, and yet I know that I should be much more sorry than glad, if he were to die: So that I am at my wit's end.

And this is what I and many others have suffered from the flute-playing of this satyr. Yet hear me once more while I show you how exact the image is, and how marvellous his power. For let me tell you; none of you know him; but I will reveal him to you; having begun, I must go on. See you how fond he is of the fair? He is always with them and is always being smitten by them, and then again he knows nothing and is ignorant of all things — such is the appearance which he puts on. Is he not like a Silenus in this? To be sure he is: His outer mask is the carved head of the Silenus; but when he is opened, what temperance there is residing within! Know you that beauty and wealth and honour, at which the many wonder, are of no account with him, and are utterly despised by him: He regards not at all the persons who are gifted with them; mankind are nothing to him; all his life is spent in mocking and flouting at them (Plato, *Symposium*, 215–16.)

## As Midwife

*The midwife image comes from a late Platonic dialogue and is in all likelihood a Platonic metaphor for the way in which philosophical interaction between student and teacher takes place. The teacher does not, to carry on the sexual metaphor, impregnate the student with his own ideas but, discovering someone who is already pregnant (with perplexity), aids in bringing the idea, like a baby, to birth. There is no guarantee that the idea is healthy, often it is stillborn (a wind-egg). Not all persons are pregnant with ideas, only someone who is labouring over a problem is ready to be assisted. In the earlier Socratic questioning mode, the respondent was led to recognize his ignorance. The maieutic method, as it is called, aims at self-knowledge.*

*Theaetetus*: But I assure you, Socrates, I have often set myself to study that problem, when I heard reports of the questions you ask. But I cannot persuade myself that I can give any satisfactory solution or that anyone has ever stated in my hearing the sort of answer you require. And yet I cannot get the question out of my mind.

*Socrates*: My dear Theaetetus, that is because your mind is not empty or barren.

You are suffering the pains of travail.

*Tht*: I don't know about that, Socrates. I am only telling you how I feel.

*Soc*: How absurd of you, never to have heard that I am the son of a midwife, a fine buxom woman called Phaenarete ('light of virtue')

*Tht*: I have heard that.

*Soc*: Have you also been told that I practise the same art?

*Tht*: No, never.

*Soc*: It is true, though; only don't give away my secret. It is not known that I possess this skill; so the ignorant world describes me in other terms as an eccentric person who reduces people to hopeless perplexity. Have you been told that too?

*Tht*. I have.

*Soc*: Shall I tell you the reason ?

*Tht*: Please do.

*Soc*: Consider, then, how it is with all midwives; that will help you to understand what I mean. I dare say you know that they never attend other women in childbirth so long as they themselves can conceive and bear children, but only when they are too old for that.

*Tht*: Of course.

*Soc*: They say that is because Artemis, the patroness of childbirth, is herself childless; and so, while she did not allow barren women to be midwives, because it is beyond the power of human nature to achieve skill without any experience, she assigned the privilege to women who were past child-bearing, out of respect to their likeness to herself.

*Tht*: That sounds likely.

*Soc*: And it is more than likely, is it not, that no one can tell so well as a midwife whether women are pregnant or not ?

*Tht*: Assuredly.

*Soc*: Moreover, with the drugs and incantations they administer, midwives can either bring on the pains of travail or allay them at their will, make a difficult labour easy, and at an early stage cause a miscarriage if they so decide.

*Tht*: True.

*Soc*: Have you also observed that they are the cleverest matchmakers, having an unerring skill in selecting a pair whose marriage will produce the best children?

*Tht*: I was not aware of that.

*Soc*: Well, you may be sure they pride themselves on that more than on cutting the umbilical cord. Consider the knowledge of the sort of plant or seed that should be sown in any given soil; does not that go together with skill in tending and harvesting the fruits of the earth? They are not two different arts?

*Tht*: No, the same.

*Soc*: And so with a woman; skill in the sowing is not to be separated from skill in the harvesting?

*Tht*: Probably not.

*Soc*: No; only, because there is that wrong and ignorant way of bringing together man and woman which they call pandering, midwives, out of self-respect, are shy even of matchmaking, for fear of falling under the accusation of pandering. Yet the genuine midwife is the only successful matchmaker.

*Tht*: That is clear.

*Soc*: All this, then, lies within the midwife's province; but her performance falls short of mine. It is not the way of women sometimes to bring forth real children, sometimes mere phantoms, such that it is hard to tell the one from the other. If it were so, the highest and noblest task of the midwife would be to discern the real from the unreal, would it not?

*Tht*: I agree.

*Soc*: My art of midwifery is in general like theirs; the only difference is that my patients are men, not women, and my concern is not with the body but with the soul that is in travail of birth. And the highest point of my art is the power to prove by every test whether the offspring of a young man's thought is a false phantom or instinct with life and truth. I am so far like the midwife, that I cannot myself give birth to wisdom; and *the common reproach is true that though I question others, I can myself bring nothing to light because there is no wisdom in me*. The reason is this: Heaven constrains me to serve as a midwife, but has debarred me from giving birth. So of myself I have no sort of wisdom, nor has any discovery ever been born to me as the child of my soul. Those who frequent my company at first appear, some of them, quite unintelligent; but, as we go further with our discussions, all who are favoured by heaven make progress at a rate that seems surprising to others as well as to themselves, although it is clear that they have never learnt anything from me; the many admirable truths they bring to birth have been discovered by themselves from within. But the delivery is heaven's work and mine. The proof of this is that many who have not been conscious of my assistance but have made light of me, thinking it was all their own doing, have left me sooner than they should, whether under others' influence or of their own motion, and *thenceforward suffered miscarriage of their thoughts through falling into bad company*. And they have lost the children of whom I had delivered them by bringing them up badly, caring more for false phantoms than for the true; and so at last their lack of understanding has become apparent to themselves and to everyone else... When they come back and beg for a renewal of our intercourse with extravagant protestations; with others it is permitted, and these begin again to make progress. In yet another way, those who seek my company have the same experience as a woman with child: they suffer the pains of labour and, by night and day, *are full of distress far greater than a woman's*; and my art has power to bring on these pangs or to allay them. So it fares with these; but there are some, Theaetetus, whose minds, as I judge, have never conceived at all. I see that they have no need of me and with all goodwill I seek a match for them...

And now for the upshot of this long discourse of mine. I suspect that, as you yourself believe, your mind is in labour with some thought it has conceived. Accept, then, the ministration of a midwife's son who himself practises his mother's art, and do the best you can to answer the questions I ask. Perhaps when I examine your statements I may judge one or another of them to be an unreal phantom. If I then take the abortion from you and cast it away, do not be savage with me like a woman robbed of her first child. People have often felt like that towards me and been positively ready to bite me for taking away some foolish notion they have conceived. They do not see that I am doing them a kindness. They have not learnt that no divinity is ever ill-disposed towards man, nor is such action on my part due to unkindness; it is only that I am not permitted to acquiesce in falsehood and suppress the truth. So, Theaetetus, start again and try to explain what knowledge is. Never say it is beyond your power; it will not be so, if heaven wills and you take courage (Plato, *Theaetetus*, 149a–151d.)

## Socrates in Aristophanes's *Clouds*

*The comic playwright Aristophanes, produced nearly 40 plays, 11 of which survive; these were produced between 427* BCE *(Plato was an infant) and 388* BCE*. The first version of the Clouds won third prize in the year 423* BCE *in the City of Dionysia (Socrates was about 45 years old, Plato about six). Aristophanes takes digs at Socrates elsewhere as well, in* The Birds, *he notes his Spartan sympathies: 'Before your city was built, all men had a mania for Sparta; long hair and fasting were held in honor, men went dirty like Socrates and carried staves.' (Birds, 1280.)*

*In the* Clouds, *Socrates is the central figure. Socrates was well-known in Athens, which is why he could be portrayed as a representative of woolly-headed thinkers. That Socrates was connected with 'thinking' (rather than, say, politically acting), is shown by the name given to his 'school' (the historical Socrates did not have any such institute), which is called the phrontesterion (or thinking place). Socrates here is presented as both a sophist (one who is able to make 'the weaker argument stronger') as well as a physical philosopher, concerned with natural elements (the Clouds) and not believing in the gods, or at least the gods the city believes in. This is not far from ideas that the early Greek physicist-philosophers held (Anaximander thought 'air' fundamental and divine). But none of these traits are attested of Socrates from other sources…*

*The play opens with an uneducated farmer Strepsiades, (so named because he 'tosses and turns' at night) and his son Pheidippides. The son is addicted to horse racing and has contracted large debts which they are unable to pay. The father suggests that he learns the art of debate so that he can win lawsuits against his creditors. He needs to learn how to make the weaker argument stronger, a claim usually made on behalf of professional sophists. The son being initially unwilling, the father goes himself to the school and meets Socrates.*

*Later there is a demonstration of how to win an argument; the arguments are themselves personified as the Just and Unjust. Here we have the initial appearance of Socrates and his conversation with the father, and the final lines at the end of the play.*

## From the *Clouds*

*Strepsiades*: Look this way then! Do you see this little door and little house?

*Pheidippides*: I see it. What then, pray, is this, father?

*Strep*: This is a thinking-shop of wise spirits. There dwell men who in speaking of the heavens persuade people that it is an oven, and that it encompasses us, and that we are the embers. These men teach, if one give them money, to conquer in speaking, right or wrong.

*Phid*: Who are they?

*Strep*: I do not know the name accurately. They are minute philosophers, noble and excellent.

*Phid*: Bah! They are rogues; I know them. You mean the quacks, the pale-faced wretches, the bare-footed fellows, of whose numbers are the miserable Socrates and Chaerephon.

*Strep*: Hold! Hold! Be silent! Do not say anything foolish. But, if you have any concern for your father's patrimony, become one of them, having given up your horsemanship.

...

*Phid*: Why, what shall I learn?

*Strep*: They say that among them are both the two causes — the better cause, whichever that is, and the worse: They say that the one of these two causes, the worse, prevails, though it speaks on the unjust side. If, therefore you learn for me this unjust cause, I would not pay anyone, not even an obol of these debts, which I owe at present on your account.

*Phid*: I can not comply.

*Exit Phidippides*.

*Strep*: Though fallen, still I will not lie prostrate: but having prayed to the gods, I will go myself to the thinking-shop and get taught. How, then, being an old man, shall I learn the subtleties of refined disquisitions? I must go. Why thus do I loiter and not knock at the door?

... knocks...

*Disciple (from within)*: Go to the devil! Who it is that knocked at the door?

*Strep*: Strepsiades, the son of Phidon, of Cicynna.

*Dis*: You are a stupid fellow, by Zeus! Who have kicked against the door so very carelessly, and have caused the miscarriage of an idea which I had conceived.

*Strep*: Pardon me; for I dwell afar in the country. But tell me the thing which has been made to miscarry.

*Dis*: It is not lawful to mention it, except to disciples.

*Strep*: Tell it, then, to me without fear; for I here am come as a disciple to the thinking-shop.

*Dis*: I will tell you; but you must regard these as mysteries. Socrates lately asked Chaerephon about a flea, how many of its own feet it jumped; for after having bit the eyebrow of Chaerephon, it leaped away onto the head of Socrates.

*Strep*: How then did he measure this?

*Dis*: Most cleverly. He melted some wax; and then took the flea and dipped its feet in the wax; and then a pair of Persian slippers stuck to it when cooled. Having gently loosened these, he measured back the distance.

*Strep*: O King Zeus! What subtlety of thought!

*Dis*: What then would you say if you heard another contrivance of Socrates?

*Strep*: Of what kind? Tell me, I beseech you!

*Dis*: Chaerephon the Sphettian asked him whether he thought gnats buzzed through the mouth or the breech.

*Strep*: What, then, did he say about the gnat?

*Dis*: He said the intestine of the gnat was narrow and that the wind went forcibly through it, being slender, straight to the breech; and then that the rump, being hollow where it is adjacent to the narrow part, resounded through the violence of the wind.

*Strep*: The rump of the gnats then is a trumpet! Oh, thrice happy he for his sharp-sightedness! Surely a defendant might easily get acquitted who understands the intestine of the gnat...Why then do we admire Thales? (*First in the list of the seven wise men*) Open open quickly the thinking-shop, and show to me Socrates as quickly as possible. For I desire to be a disciple. Come, open the door.

The door of the thinking-shop opens and the pupils of Socrates are seen all with their heads fixed on the ground, while Socrates himself is seen suspended in the air in a basket.

O Hercules, from what country are these wild beasts... But why in the world do these look upon the ground?

*Dis*: They are in search of the things below the earth.

*Strep*: Then they are searching for roots. Do not, then, trouble yourselves about this; for I know where there are large and fine ones. Why, what are these doing, who are bent down so much?

*Dis*: These are groping about in darkness under Tartarus.

*Strep*: Why then does their rump look toward heaven?

*Dis*: It is getting taught astronomy alone by itself.

...

*Strep* (discovering a variety of mathematical instruments): Why, what is this, in the name of heaven? Tell me.

*Dis*: This is Astronomy.

*Strep*: But what is this?

*Dis*: Geometry.

*Strep*: What then is the use of this?

*Dis*: To measure out the land.

*Strep*: You tell me a clever notion; for the contrivance is democratic and useful.

*Dis (pointing to a map)*: See, here's a map of the whole earth. Do you see? This is Athens.

*Strep*: What say you? I don't believe you; for I do not see the Dicasts (jurors) sitting.

*Dis*: Be assured that this is truly the Attic territory.

*Strep*: ...But where is Lacedaemon (Sparta)?

*Dis*: Where is it? Here it is.

*Strep*: How near it is to us! Pay great attention to this, to remove it very far from us.

*Dis*: By Zeus, it is not possible.

*Strep*: Then you will weep for it.

*Looking up and discovering Socrates.*

Come, who is this man who is in the basket?

*Dis*: Himself.

*Strep*: Who's Himself?

*Dis*: Socrates.

*Strep*: O Socrates! Come, you sir, call upon him loudly for me.

*Dis*: Nay, rather, call him yourself; for I have no leisure.

*Exit Disciple.*

*Strep*: Socrates! My little Socrates!

Socrates Why callest thou me, thou creature of a day?

*Strep*: First tell me, I beseech you, what are you doing.

*Soc*: I am walking in the air, and speculating about the sun.

*Strep*: And so you look down upon the gods from your basket, and not from the earth?

*Soc*: For I should not have rightly discovered things celestial if I had not suspended the intellect, and mixed the thought in a subtle form with its kindred air. But if, being on the ground, I speculated from below on things above, I should never have discovered them. For the earth forcibly attracts to itself the meditative moisture. ...

*Strep*: ...Come then, my little Socrates, descend to me, that you may teach me those things, for the sake of which I have come.

*Socrates lowers himself and gets out of the basket.*

*Soc*: And for what did you come?

*Strep*: Wishing to learn to speak; for by reason of usury, and most ill-natured creditors, I am pillaged and plundered, and have my goods seized for debt.

*Soc*: How did you get in debt without observing it?

*Strep*: A horse-disease consumed me—terrible at eating. But teach me the other one of your two causes, that which pays nothing; and I will swear by the gods, I will pay down to you whatever reward you exact of me.

*Soc*: By what gods will you swear? For, in the first place, gods are not a current coin with us.

*Strep*: By what do you swear? By iron money, as in Byzantium?

*Soc*: Do you wish to know clearly celestial matters, what they rightly are?

*Strep*: Yes, by Zeus, if it be possible.

*Soc*: And to hold converse with the Clouds, our divinities?

*Strep*: By all means.

*Soc (with great solemnity)*: Seat yourself, then, upon the sacred couch…

*Strep*: Then what shall I gain, pray?

*Soc*: You shall become in oratory a tricky knave, a thorough rattle, a subtle speaker. But keep quiet.

*At the end of the Play, Strepsiades and his son quarrel. The son, having learnt how to make the weaker argument stronger convinces his father that it is right for children to beat their own fathers. Regretting that he had his son schooled in the New Morality, Strepsiades blames Socrates and sets his school (the phrontesterion) on fire, smoking him out, 'for his crime against the gods'.*

*Strep*: Ah me, what madness! How mad, then, I was when I ejected the gods on account of Socrates! But O dear Hermes, by no means be wroth with me, nor destroy me; but pardon me, since I have gone crazy through prating. And become my adviser, whether I shall bring an action and prosecute them, or whatever you think. You advise me rightly, not permitting me to get up a lawsuit, but as soon as possible to set fire to the house of the prating fellows... But let some one bring me a lighted torch and I'll make some of them this day suffer punishment, even if they be ever so much impostors...

*Dis*: What are you doing, fellow?

*Strep*: What am I doing? Why, what else, than chopping logic with the beams of your house?

*Sets the house on fire*

*Soc (from within)*: Hollo you! What are you doing, pray, you fellow on the roof?

*Strep*: I am walking on air, and speculating about the sun.

*Soc*: Ah me, unhappy! I shall be suffocated, wretched man!

*Chaerophon*: And I, miserable man, shall be burnt to death!

*Strep*: For what has come into your heads that you acted insolently toward the gods, and pried into the seat of the moon? Chase, pelt, smite them, for many reasons, but especially because you know that they offended against the gods! (Aristophanes, *Clouds*, selections.)

*The thinking-shop is burned down.*

# 3

## SLAVE TO THE GODS

### *His Daimon. On Piety. Serving the Gods.*

*Socrates was charged with impiety: not believing in the gods of the city but introducing strange new gods. Xenophon's Memorablia opens with a summary of the charges against him:*

The indictment against him was to this effect: Socrates is guilty of rejecting the gods acknowledged by the state and of bringing in strange deities: He is also guilty of corrupting the youth.

First then, that he rejected the gods acknowledged by the state what evidence did they produce of that? He offered sacrifices constantly, and made no secret of it, now in his home, now at the altars of the state temples, and he made use of divination with as little secrecy. Indeed it had become notorious that Socrates claimed to be guided by 'the deity' (*daimonion*) it was out of this claim, I think, that the charge of bringing in strange deities arose. (*Memorabilia,* 1.1.)

*Socrates was no atheist, his belief in a tutelary deity, his 'daimonion' or guardian spirit was not antithetical to his times, the very word for happiness eudaimonia, literally means having a good (guiding) spirit. The city-states had their own presiding deities and public and private rituals were very much a part of civic life. It was after all the oracle of Apollo at Delphi that pronounced Socrates the wisest man in Greece. The mission that Socrates undertakes is one which he says is god-given.*

## His Daimon

*One of the accusations brought against Socrates was that he worshipped strange deities. This referred to the 'diamonion' or guiding spirit that is frequently mentioned in all the sources. There was much speculation over what exactly it was, a voice or some internal impulse. Critics are divided over whether it is the voice of reason, or an extra-rational external command. But while it was unique to Socrates, his belief in the truth of oracles and dreams, accords well with the outlook of his times. There were different accounts on whether it merely prevented some course of action or actively encouraged Socrates. In Plato's version it only occasionally prevents Socrates from doing something.*

*Socrates*: Perhaps it may seem strange that I go about and interfere in other people's affairs to give this advice in private, but do not venture to come before your assembly and advise the state. But the reason for this, as you have heard me say at many times and places, is that something divine and spiritual comes to me, the very thing which Meletus ridiculed in his indictment. I have had this from my childhood; it is a sort of voice that comes to me, and when it comes it always holds me back from what I am thinking of doing, but never urges me forward. This 'it' is which opposes my engaging in politics. (Plato, *Apology*, 31c.)

*Socrates can also talk as if he were a seer, looking into and predicting future events. This is at odds with his central claim that he does not know (anything). He also seems, in Xenophon's account, to accept the power of dreams to predict future events. He describes the art of the seer as 'more perfect and more admirable' than the art of prediction from birds. The* Theages, *a dialogue, thought in antiquity to be an early platonic composition but now considered to be the work by someone else well-versed in Socratic-Platonic writing, presents Socrates as being guided by his inner voice to foresee future disasters that will befall both individuals and cities. In short, Socrates is cast here as a guru, rather than a seeker after wisdom.*

*Socrates*: For there is something demonic which, by divine dispensation, has accompanied me from childhood, a voice which, when it occurs, always indicates a prohibition of something I may be about to do, but never urges me on to anything; and if one of my friends consults me and the voice occurs, the same thing happens: It prohibits, and does not allow him to act. And I will produce witnesses to convince you of these facts. You know our Charmides here, who has grown so handsome, he once happened to be consulting me that he was going to train to race for the Nemean races, and immediately when he began to say that, the voice came; I opposed him and said: As you were speaking the voice came to me, no don't train.

— Probably, he said, it signals to you that I shall not win; but even if I am not going to win, the exercise I will get during this time, will do me good. So saying, he trained; now it's worth hearing from him the things that befell him on account of this training.

...Moreover, concerning the Sicilian business (the destruction of the Athenian army in 415 BCE), you will hear from many the things I said about the destruction of the expedition. And as regards things that are past, it is possible to hear from those who know; but it is also possible to make trial now of the sign, to see if it does say anything. For when the handsome Sannio went out on campaign the sign came to me, and he is now on an expedition with Thrasyllus against Ephesus and lonia. I accordingly expect he will either be killed or undergo something similar to this, at any rate, and I am in great fear for the sake of the rest of the army. (Plato, *Theages*, 128d, 129d.)

**Slave to God**

*As recounted by Plato, Socrates, as he cheerfully awaits his execution, describes himself as a slave to god.*

*Freedom-loving Athenians routinely contrasted their cherished freedom with the status of slaves. To be a slave was to lack independence. Persia was often described as a country where only one man (the king) was free. While the Spartans considered themselves 'slaves to the laws', Socrates's self-description underscores his total submission to the divine just before his death.*

*Socrates*: Ah, Simmias! I should have hard work to persuade other people that I do not regard my present situation as a misfortune, when I cannot even make you believe it, but you are afraid I am more churlish now than I used to be. And you seem to think I am inferior in prophetic power to the swans who sing at other times also, but when they feel that they are to die, sing most and best in their joy that they are to go to the god whose servants they are. But men, because of their own fear of death, misrepresent the swans and say that they sing for sorrow, in mourning for their own death. They do not consider that no bird sings when it is hungry or cold or has any other trouble; no, not even the nightingale or the swallow or the hoopoe which are said to sing in lamentation. I do not believe they sing for grief, nor do the swans; but since they are Apollo's birds, I believe they have prophetic vision, and because they have foreknowledge of the blessings in the other world they sing and rejoice on that day more than ever before. And I think that I am myself a fellow-slave of the swans, and am consecrated to the same God and have received from our master a gift of prophecy no whit inferior to theirs, and that I go out from life with as little sorrow as they. So far as this is concerned, then, speak and ask whatever questions you please, so long as the Eleven of the Athenians permit. (Plato, *Phaedo*, 84e–85b.)

*An early version of the argument from design is attributed to Socrates by Xenophon.*

I will first state what I once heard him say about the godhead in conversation with Aristodemus the dwarf, as he was called. On learning that he was not known to sacrifice or pray or use divination, and actually made a mock of those who did so, he said:

*Socrates*: Tell me, Aristodemus, do you admire any human beings for wisdom?

— I do, he answered.

— tell us their names.

— In epic poetry Homer comes first, in my opinion; in dithyramb, Melanippides; in tragedy, Sophocles; in sculpture, Polycleitus; in painting, Zeuxis.

— Which, think you, deserve the greater admiration, the creators of phantoms without sense and motion, or the creators of living, intelligent, and active beings?

— Oh, of living beings, by far, provided only they are created by design and not mere chance.

— Suppose that it is impossible to guess the purpose of one creature's existence, and obvious that another's serves a useful end, which, in your judgment, is the work of chance, and which of design?

— Presumably the creature that serves some useful end is the work of design.

— Do you not think then that he who created man from the beginning had some useful end in view when he endowed him with his several senses, giving eyes to see visible objects, ears to hear sounds? Again, the incisors of all creatures are adapted for cutting, the molars for receiving food from them and grinding it... With such signs of forethought in these arrangements, can you doubt whether they are the works of chance or design?

— No, of course not. When I regard them in this light they do look very like the handiwork of a wise and loving creator.

— as for mind... do you think that you snapped it up by a lucky accident, and that the orderly ranks of all these huge masses, infinite in number, are due, forsooth, to a sort of absurdity?

— Yes; for I don't see the master hand, whereas I see the makers of things in this world.

— Neither do you see your own soul, which has the mastery of the body; so that, as far as that goes, you may say that you do nothing by design, but everything by chance.

Here Aristodemus exclaimed: Really, Socrates, I don't despise the godhead. But I think it is too great to need my service.

— Then the greater the power that deigns to serve you, the more honour it demands of you.

— I assure yon, that if I believed that the gods pay any heed to man, I would not neglect them.

— Then do you think them unheeding? In the first place, man is the only living creature that they have caused to stand upright; and the upright position gives him a wider range of vision in front and a better view of things above, and exposes him less to injury. Secondly, to grovelling creatures they have given feet that afford only the power of moving, whereas they have endowed man with hands, which are the instruments to which we chiefly owe our greater happiness. Again, though all creatures have a tongue, the tongue of man alone has been formed by them to be capable of contact with different parts of the mouth, so as to enable us to articulate the voice and express all our wants to one another. Once more, for all other creatures they have prescribed a fixed season of sexual indulgence; in our case the only time limit they have set is old age...

Nor was the deity content to care for man's body. What is of yet higher moment, he has implanted in him the noblest type of soul. For in the first place what other creature's soul has apprehended the existence of gods who set in order the universe, greatest and fairest of things? And what race of living things other than man worships gods? What are they to do, to make you believe that they are heedful of you ?

— I will believe when they send counsellors, as you declare they do, saying, do this, avoid that.

— But when the Athenians inquire of them by divination and they reply, do you not suppose that to you, too, the answer is given? Or when they send portents for warning to the Greeks, or to all the world? Are you their one exception, the only one consigned to neglect? Or do you suppose that the gods would have put into man a belief in their ability to help and harm, if they had not that power; and that man throughout the ages would never have detected the fraud? Do you not see that the wisest and most enduring of human institutions, cities, and nations, are most god-fearing, and that the most thoughtful period of life is the most religious? Be well-assured, my good friend, that the mind within you directs your body according to its will; and equally you must think that Thought indwelling in the Universal disposes all things according to its pleasure... Nay, but just as by serving men you find out who is willing to serve you in return, by being kind who will be kind to you in return, and by taking counsel, discover the masters of thought, so try the gods by serving them, and see whether they will vouchsafe to counsel you in matters hidden from man. Then you will know that such is the greatness and such the nature of the deity that he sees all things and hears all things alike, and is present in all places and heedful of all things. (Xenophon, *Memorabilia*, 2.4.2–18.)

## Socrates on Piety or Holiness

*Socrates was not the only thinker who was charged with impiety or sacrilege. Around 430* BCE, *disbelief in the supernatural and the teaching of astronomy were made indictable offences. Before Socrates, Diagoras was condemned but fled Athens in 414* BCE. *The chorus in Aristophanes's* The Birds *sings: 'I hear it proclaimed: A talent (a very large sum of money) for him who shall kill Diagoras of Melos.' The philosopher Anaxagoras, who declared that the sun was a rock, was exiled; Protagoras and Euripides left Athens for similar reasons. Aristotle, after the death of Alexander the Great, fearing prosecution, left in 322* BCE. *In many of these cases there was most likely a political angle as well. But then politics uses religious ideology whenever it can.*

*In Plato's dialogue, the Euthyphro, Socrates, en route to the court of the King-Archon (the appointed civil magistrate was so named), to answer the charge of impiety, meets with Euthyphro, a seer and mantic (his name, ironically, means 'straight-thinker'). Euthyphro claims to be an expert on piety and holiness. Socrates questions him about piety. Euthyphro fails to provide answers that resist Socratic examination. Although the dialogue ends inconclusively, with no satisfactory definition arrived at, in the course of the conversation, we get a glimpse of Socrates's radical theology, independent of the popular understanding of obligations to the gods. Using a grammatical distinction between active and passive forms of verbs ('carries' as opposed to 'is carried'), Socrates undermines an everyday understanding of piety. We will take up the initial characterization of piety that Euthyphro offers and Socrates's response. Thereafter Euthyphro's second revised account (or definition) and Socrates's rebuttal.*

*Socrates*: But I will amend the definition so far as to say that what all the gods hate is impious, and what they love pious or holy... Shall this be our definition of piety and impiety?

*Euthyphro*: Yes, I should say that what all the gods love is pious and holy, and the opposite which they all hate, impious.

*Soc*: Ought we to enquire into the truth of this, Euthyphro, or simply to accept the mere statement on our own authority and that of others? What do you say?

*Euth*: We should enquire; and I believe that the statement will stand the test of enquiry.

*Soc*: We shall know better, my good friend, in a little while. The point which I should first wish to understand is whether the pious or holy is beloved by the gods because it is holy, or holy because it is beloved of the gods.

*Euth*: I do not understand your meaning, Socrates.

*Soc*: I will endeavour to explain: We, speak of carrying and we speak of being carried, of leading and being led, seeing and being seen. You know that in all such cases there is a difference, and you know also in what the difference lies?

*Euth*: I think that I understand.

*Soc*: And is not that which is beloved distinct from that which loves?

*Euth*: Certainly.

*Soc*: Well; and now tell me, is that which is carried in this state of carrying because it is carried, or for some other reason?

*Euth*: No; that is the reason.

*Soc*: And the same is true of what is led and of what is seen?

*Euth*: True.

*Soc*: And a thing is not seen because it is visible, but conversely, visible because it is seen; nor is a thing led because it is in the state of being led, or carried because it is in the state of being carried, but the converse of this. And now I think, Euthyphro, that my meaning will be intelligible; and my meaning is, that any state of action or passion implies previous action or passion. It does not become because it is becoming, but it is in a state of becoming because it becomes; neither does it suffer because it is in a state of suffering, but it is in a state of suffering because it suffers.

Do you not agree?

*Euth*: Yes.

*Soc*: Is not that which is loved in some state either of becoming or suffering?

*Euth*: Yes.

*Soc*: And the same holds as in the previous instances; the state of being loved follows the act of being loved, and not the act the state.

*Euth*: Certainly.

*Soc*: And what do you say of piety, Euthyphro: is not piety, according to your definition, loved by all the gods?

*Euth*: Yes.

*Soc*: Because it is pious or holy, or for some other reason?

*Euth*: No, that is the reason.

*Soc*: It is loved because it is holy, not holy because it is loved?

*Euth*: Yes.

*Soc*: And that which is dear to the gods is loved by them, and is in a state to be loved of them because it is loved of them?

*Euth*: Certainly.

*Soc*: Then that which is dear to the gods, Euthyphro, is not holy, nor is that which is holy loved of God, as you affirm; but they are two different things.

*Euth*: How do you mean, Socrates?

*Soc*: I mean to say that the holy has been acknowledged by us to be loved of God because it is holy, not to be holy because it is loved.

*Euth*: Yes.

*Soc*: But that which is dear to the gods is dear to them because it is loved by them, not loved by them because it is dear to them.

*Euth*: True.

*Soc*: But, friend Euthyphro, if that which is holy is the same with that which is dear to God, and is loved because it is holy, then that which is dear to God would have been loved as being dear to God. But if that which is dear to God is dear to him because it is loved by him, then that which is holy would have been holy because it is loved by him. But now you see that the reverse is the case, and that they are quite different from one another. For one (theophiles, god-loved) is of a kind to be loved because it is loved, and the other (hosion, holy) is loved because it is of a kind to be loved. Thus you appear to me, Euthyphro when I ask you what is the essence of holiness, to offer an attribute only, and not the essence — the attribute of being loved by all the gods. But you still refuse to explain to me the nature of holiness. And therefore, if you please, I will ask you not to hide your treasure, but to tell me once more what holiness or piety really is, whether dear to the gods or not (for that is a matter about which we will not quarrel); and what is impiety?

*Euth*: I really do not know, Socrates, how to express what I mean. For somehow or other our arguments, on whatever ground we rest them, seem to turn round and walk away from us.

*Soc*: Your words, Euthyphro, are like the handiwork of my ancestor Daedalus; and if I were the sayer or propounder of them, you might say that my arguments walk away and will not remain fixed where they are placed because I am a descendant of his. But now, since these notions are your own, you must find some other gibe, for they certainly, as you yourself allow, show an inclination to be on the move.

*Euth*: Nay, Socrates, I shall still say that you are the Daedalus who sets arguments in motion; not I, certainly, but you make them move or go round, for they would never have stirred, as far as I am concerned. (Plato, *Euthyphro*, 9e–11d)

## Serving the Gods

*While it may (or must) be true that the pious is loved by all the gods, that cannot be the reason why what they love (in general or particular acts), is pious. Merely because everyone (e.g. the Athenians) think that some things are pious and some impious, does not make them pious or holy. The answer to the question of piety is not to be found in what most or even all people think. It does not matter whether all or some of the gods (or for that matter, men) love and approve of something, unless they approve of it because it is worthy of approval (i.e. good). If the Greek gods, like men, disagree about what is good, numbers cannot decide what is good or worthy of approval, but a standard, independent of them. Socrates's logical observation, separating cause from consequence and essence from accident is a profound critique of unthinking religious beliefs. Euthyphro, with some help from Socrates, offers a revised definition of piety. Euthyphro's conception of piety, like that of many others, sees it as a transactional business arrangement between men and gods.*

*Euthyphro*: Piety or holiness, Socrates, appears to me to be that part of justice which attends to the gods, as there is the other part of justice which attends to men.

*Soc*: That is good, Euthyphro; yet still there is a little point about which I should like to have further information. What is the meaning of 'attention'? For 'attention' can hardly be used in the same sense when applied to the gods as when applied to other things. For instance, horses are said to require attention, and not every person is able to attend to them, but only a person skilled in horsemanship. Is it not so?

*Euth*: Certainly.

*Soc*: I should suppose that the art of horsemanship is the art of attending to horses?

*Euth*: Yes.

*Soc*: Nor is every one qualified to attend to dogs, but only the huntsman?

*Euth*: True.

*Soc*: And I should also conceive that the art of the huntsman is the art of attending to dogs?

*Euth*: Very true.

*Soc*: In like manner holiness or piety is the art of attending to the gods — that would be your meaning?

*Euth*: Yes.

*Soc*: And is not attention always designed for the good or benefit of that to which the attention is given? As in the case of horses, you may observe that when attended to by the horseman's art they are benefited and improved, are they not?

*Euth*: True.

*Soc*: ...And all other things are tended or attended for their good and not for their hurt?

*Euth*: Certainly, not for their hurt.

*Soc*: But for their good?

*Euth*: Of course.

*Soc*: And does piety or holiness, which has been defined to be the art of attending to the gods, benefit or improve them? Would you say that when you do a holy act you make any of the gods better?

*Euth*: No, no; that was certainly not what I meant.

*Soc*: Good, but I must still ask what is this attention to the gods which is called piety?

*Euth*: It is such, Socrates, as servants show to their masters.

*Soc*: I understand — a sort of ministration to the gods.

*Euth*: Exactly.

*Soc*: Medicine is also a sort of ministration or service, having in view the attainment of some object—would you not say of health?

*Euth*: I should.

*Soc*: And now tell me, my good friend, about the art which ministers to the gods: What work does that help to accomplish? ...What is that fair work which the gods do by the help of our ministrations?

*Euth*: Many and fair, Socrates, are the works which they do.

*Soc*: Why, my friend, and so are those of a general. But the chief of them is easily told. Would you not say that victory in war is the chief of them?

*Euth*: Certainly.

*Soc*: And of the many and fair things done by the gods, which is the chief or principal one?

*Euth*: I have told you already, Socrates, that to learn all these things accurately will be very tiresome. Let me simply say that piety or holiness is learning how to please the gods in word and deed, by prayers and sacrifices. Such piety is the salvation of families and states, just as the impious, which is unpleasing to the gods, is their ruin and destruction.

*Soc*: I think that you could have answered in much fewer words the chief question which I asked, Euthyphro, if you had chosen... Do you mean that they are a sort of science of praying and sacrificing?

*Euth*: Yes, I do.

*Soc*: And sacrificing is giving to the gods, and prayer is asking of the gods?

*Euth*: Yes, Socrates.

*Soc*: Upon this view, then, piety is a science of asking and giving?

*Euth*: You understand me capitally, Socrates.

*Soc*: ...Please then to tell me, what is the nature of this service to the gods? Do you mean that we prefer requests and give gifts to them?

*Euth*: Yes, I do.

*Soc*: Is not the right way of asking to ask of them what we want?

*Euth*: Certainly.

*Soc*: And the right way of giving is to give to them in return what they want of us.

There would be no meaning in an art which gives to anyone that which he does not want.

*Euth*: Very true, Socrates.

*Soc*: Then piety, Euthyphro, is an art which gods and men have of doing business with one another?

*Euth*: That is an expression which you may use, if you like.

*Soc*: But I have no particular liking for anything but the truth. I wish, however, that you would tell me what benefit accrues to the gods from our gifts. There is no doubt about what they give to us; *for there is no good thing which they do not give*; but how we can give any good thing to them in return is far from being equally clear.

If they give everything and we give nothing, that must be an affair of business in which we have very greatly the advantage of them.

*Euth*: And do you imagine, Socrates, that any benefit accrues to the gods from our gifts?

*Soc*: But if not, Euthyphro, what is the meaning of gifts which are conferred by us upon the gods?

*Euth*: What else, but tributes of honour; and, as I was just now saying, what pleases them?

*Soc*: Piety, then, is pleasing to the gods, but not beneficial or dear to them?

*Euth*: I should say that nothing could be dearer.

*Soc*: Then once more the assertion is repeated that piety is dear to the gods?

*Euth*: Certainly.

*Soc*: And when you say this, can you wonder at your words not standing firm, but walking away? Will you accuse me of being the Daedalus who makes them walk away, not perceiving that there is another and far greater artist than Daedalus who makes them go round in a circle, and he is yourself. For the argument, as you will perceive, comes round to the same point. Were we not saying that the holy or pious was not the same with that which is loved of the gods? Have you forgotten?

*Euth*: I quite remember.

*Soc*: And are you not saying that what is loved of the gods is holy; and is not this the same as what is dear to them — do you see?

*Euth*: True.

*Soc*: Then either we were wrong in our former assertion; or, if we were right then, we are wrong now.

*Euth*: One of the two must be true.

*Soc*: Then we must begin again and ask: What is piety? That is an enquiry which I shall never be weary of pursuing as far as in me lies; and I entreat you not to scorn me, but to apply your mind to the utmost, and tell me the truth... Speak out then, my dear Euthyphro, and do not hide your knowledge.

*Euth*: Another time, Socrates; for I am in a hurry, and must go now.

*Soc*: Alas! my companion, and will you leave me in despair? I was hoping that you would instruct me in the nature of piety and impiety; and then I might have cleared myself of Meletus and his indictment. I would have told him that I had been enlightened by Euthyphro, and had given up rash innovations and speculations, in which I indulged only through ignorance, and that now I am about to lead a better life. (Plato, *Euthyphro*, 12e–16a.)

# 4

# IN PRISON

## *No Escaping Justice. Obedience to the Laws.*

*Following his death sentence, Socrates was imprisoned for almost a month, unusual for the Athenian legal system, where the implementation of the death penalty was carried out without delay. But when Socrates lost his case, no executions could be carried out. This had the effect of giving Socrates an extra month of life, which he spent in prison. The reason for the delay is spelled out in the opening conversation of the Phaedo, in which Plato recounts the day of Socrates's execution.*

*Echecrates*: Were you with Socrates yourself, Phaedo, on the day when he drank the poison in prison, or did you hear about it from someone else?

*Phaedo*: Did you not even hear about the trial and how it was conducted?

*Echecrates*: Yes, someone told us about that, and we wondered that although it took place a long time ago, he was put to death much later. Now why was that, Phaedo?

*Phaedo*: It was a matter of chance, Echecrates. It happened that the stern of the ship which the Athenians send to Delos was crowned on the day before the trial.

*Echecrates*: What ship is this?

*Phaedo*: This is the ship, as the Athenians say, in which Theseus once went to Crete with the fourteen youths and maidens and saved them and himself. Now the Athenians made a vow to Apollo, as the story goes, that if they were saved they would send a mission every year to Delos. And from that time even to the present day they send it annually in honor of the god. Now it is their law that after the mission begins the city must be pure and no one may be publicly executed until the ship has gone to Delos and back; and sometimes, when contrary winds detain it, this takes a long time. The beginning of the mission is when the priest of Apollo crowns the stern of the ship; and this took place, as I say, on the day before the trial. For that reason Socrates passed a long time in prison between his trial and his death. (Plato, *Phaedo*, 57a–58c.)

## Escape from Prison

*While he was imprisoned, Socrates's friends had organized his escape by bribing the guards, and arranging for him to leave the city. The dialogue opens with Crito arriving at the prison on the morning of the day he thinks Socrates will be killed. Socrates however corrects him: A vision, quoting Homer, appeared to him while asleep, (the lines foretold the death of Achilles), that he will die on the third day. Socrates was executed mid-February 399 BCE.*

*Socrates*: Why have you come at this hour, Crito? it must be quite early.

*Crito*: Yes, certainly.

*Soc*: What is the exact time?

*Cr*: The dawn is breaking.

*Soc*: I wonder if the keeper of the prison would let you in.

*Cr*: He knows me because I often come, Socrates; moreover, I have done him a kindness.

*Soc*: And are you only just come?

*Cr*: No, I came some time ago.

*Soc*: Then why did you sit and say nothing, instead of awakening me at once?

*Cr*: Why, indeed, Socrates, I myself would rather not have all this sleeplessness and sorrow. But I have been wondering at your peaceful slumbers, and that was the reason why I did not awaken you, because I wanted you to be out of pain. I have always thought you happy in the calmness of your temperament; but never did I see the like of the easy, cheerful way in which you bear this calamity.

*Soc*: Why, Crito, when a man has reached my age he ought not to be repining at the prospect of death.

*Cr*: And yet other old men find themselves in similar misfortunes, and age does not prevent them from repining.

*Soc*: That may be. But you have not told me why you come at this early hour.

*Cr*: I come to bring you a message which is sad and painful; not, as I believe, to yourself but to all of us who are your friends, and saddest of all to me.

*Soc*: What! I suppose that the ship has come from Delos, on the arrival of which I am to die?

*Cr*: No, the ship has not actually arrived, but she will probably be here today, as persons who have come from Sunium tell me that they have left her there; and therefore tomorrow, Socrates, will be the last day of your life.

*Soc*: Very well, Crito, if such is the will of God, I am willing; but my belief is that there will be a delay of a day.

*Cr*: Why do you say this?

*Soc*: I will tell you. I am to die on the day after the arrival of the ship?

*Cr*: Yes; that is what the authorities say.

*Soc*: But I do not think that the ship will be here until tomorrow; this I gather from a vision which I had last night, or rather only just now, when you fortunately allowed me to sleep.

*Cr*: And what was the nature of the vision?

*Soc*: There came to me the likeness of a woman, fair and comely, clothed in white raiment, who called to me and said: O Socrates:

"The third day hence, to Phthia shalt thou go."

*Cr*: What a singular dream, Socrates!

*Soc*: There can be no doubt about the meaning Crito, I think.

*Cr*: Yes, the meaning is only too clear. But, O! my beloved Socrates, let me entreat you once more to take my advice and escape. For if you die I shall not only lose a friend who can never be replaced, but there is another evil: People who do not know you and me will believe that I might have saved you if I had been willing to give money, but that I did not care. Now, can there be a worse disgrace than this — that I should be thought to value money more than the life of a friend? For the many will not be persuaded that I wanted you to escape, and that you refused.

*Soc*: But why, my dear Crito, should we care about the opinion of the many? Good men, and they are the only persons who are worth considering, will think of these things truly as they happened.

*Cr*: But do you see. Socrates, that the opinion of the many must be regarded, as is evident in your own case, because they can do the very greatest evil to anyone who has lost their good opinion?

*Soc*: I only wish, Crito, that they could; for then they could also do the greatest good, and that would be well. But the truth is, that they can do neither good nor evil: They cannot make a man wise or make him foolish, and whatever they do is the result of chance…

*Soc*: Dear Crito, your zeal is invaluable, if a right one; but if wrong, the greater the zeal the greater the evil; and therefore we ought to consider whether these things shall be done or not. For I am and always have been one of those natures who must be guided by reason, whatever the reason may be which upon reflection appears to me to be the best; and now that this fortune has come upon me, I cannot put away the reasons which I have before given: The principles which I have hitherto honoured and revered I still honour, and unless we can find other and better principles on the instant, I am certain not to agree with you; no, not even if the power of the multitude could inflict many more imprisonments, confiscations, deaths, frightening us like children with hobgoblin terrors. But what will be the fairest way of considering the question? Shall I return to your old argument about the opinions of men, some of which are to be regarded, and others, as we were saying, are not to be regarded?

Now you, Crito, are a disinterested person who are not going to die tomorrow — at least, there is no human probability of this, and you are therefore not liable to be deceived by the circumstances in which you are placed. Tell me, then, whether I am right in saying that some opinions, and the opinions of some men only, are to be valued, and other opinions, and the opinions of other men, are not to be valued. I ask you whether I was right in maintaining this?

*Cr*: Certainly.

*Soc*: The good are to be regarded, and not the bad?

*Cr*: Yes.

*Soc*: And the opinions of the wise are good, and the opinions of the unwise are evil?

*Cr*: Certainly.

*Soc*: And what was said about another matter? Was the disciple in gymnastics supposed to attend to the praise and blame and opinion of every man, or of one man only — his physician or trainer, whoever that was?

*Cr*: Of one man only.

*Soc*: And he ought to fear the censure and welcome the praise of that one only, and not of the many?

*Cr*: That is clear.

*Soc*: And he ought to live and train, and eat and drink in the way which seems good to his single master who has understanding, rather than according to the opinion of all other men put together?

*Cr*: True.

*Soc*: And if he disobeys and disregards the opinion and approval of the one, and regards the opinion of the many who have no understanding, will he not suffer evil?

*Cr*: Certainly he will.

*Soc*: And what will the evil be, whither tending and what affecting, in the disobedient person?

*Cr*: Clearly, affecting the body; that is what is destroyed by the evil.

*Soc*: Very good; and is not this true, Crito, of other things which we need not separately enumerate? In the matter of just and unjust, fair and foul, good and evil, which are the subjects of our present consultation, ought we to follow the opinion of the many and to fear them; or the opinion of the one man who has understanding, and whom we ought to fear and reverence more than all the rest of the world: and whom deserting we shall destroy and injure that principle in us which may be assumed to be improved by justice and deteriorated by injustice; is there not such a principle?

*Cr*: Certainly there is, Socrates.

*Soc*: Take a parallel instance; if, acting under the advice of men who have no understanding, we destroy that which is improvable by health and deteriorated by disease — when that has been destroyed, I say, would life be worth having? And that is — the body?

*Cr*: Yes.

*Soc*: Could we live, having an evil and corrupted body?

*Cr*: Certainly not.

*Soc*: And will life be worth having, if that higher part of man be depraved, which is improved by justice and deteriorated by injustice? Do we suppose that principle, whatever it may be in man, which has to do with justice and injustice, to be inferior to the body?

*Cr*: Certainly not.

*Soc*: Then, my friend, we must not regard what the many say of us: But what he, the one man who has understanding of just and unjust, will say, and what the truth will say. And therefore you begin in error when you suggest that we should regard the opinion of the many about just and unjust, good and evil, honourable and dishonourable. Well, someone will say, 'But the many can kill us.'

*Cr*: Yes, Socrates; that will clearly be the answer.

*Soc*: That is true; but still I find with surprise that the old argument is, as I conceive, unshaken as ever. And I should like to know whether I may say the same of another proposition: that not life, but a good life, is to be chiefly valued?

*Cr*: Yes, that also remains.

*Soc*: And a good life is equivalent to a just and honorable one- that holds also?

*Cr*: Yes, that holds.

*Soc*: From these premises *I proceed to argue the question whether I ought or ought not to try to escape without the consent of the Athenians:* and if I am clearly right in escaping, then I will make the attempt; but if not, I will abstain. (Plato, *Crito*, 42a–48c.)

## Obedience to the Laws

*In his conversation with Crito, Socrates goes to great lengths to defend the idea of obedience to law. He seems to claim that no matter what the city commands, a citizen is bound to obey. In the context of his own sentence, he refuses to disobey the court's order by escaping, arguing that that would amount to the very destruction of the legal system. Commentators have been divided about how literally his defence of law is to be read. After all, he did not follow the unjust orders of the Thirty in the case of Leon. He might have been punished then if the oligarchy had not been overthrown. In the case of the generals, he voted against popular sentiment because he thought it unjust. In that instance he was unable to persuade those who condemned the six generals. In his own case, he was unable to persuade the jury of his innocence, Yet he did note that if he was released on the condition that he ceased his philosophical activities, he would disobey, and thereby implicitly agreed to accept the punishment that that would invite. Socrates here does not make any appeal to a divine law, in conflict with the legal procedures adopted in the democratic city.*

*The dialogue that follows has the personified Laws convincing Socrates that he has been brought up and nurtured by them and therefore implicitly made a contract with them, and so cannot disobey them. If he must act contrary to the law, he must use persuasion, that is argument, to convince them that what they command is unjust. Since he has accepted, indeed invited the penalty of death, he cannot now avoid it by escaping from prison. Plato has constructed a dialogue within a dialogue.*

*Socrates*: Then consider the matter in this way: Imagine that I am about to play truant (you may call the proceeding by any name which you like), and the laws and the government come and interrogate me:

— 'Tell us, Socrates, they say; what are you about? Are you going by an act of yours to overturn us.

— The laws and the whole State, as far as in you lies? Do you imagine that a State can subsist and not be overthrown, in which the decisions of law have no power, but are set aside and overthrown by individuals?

— What will be our answer, Crito, to these and the like words? Anyone, and especially a clever rhetorician, will have a good deal to urge about the evil of setting aside the law which requires a sentence to be carried out. And we might reply: Yes, but the State has injured us and given an unjust sentence. Suppose I say that?

*Crito*: Very good, Socrates.

— And was that our agreement with you? the law would say, or were you to abide by the sentence of the State?

*Soc*: And if I were to express astonishment at their saying this, the law would probably add:

— Answer, Socrates, you are in the habit of asking and answering questions. Tell us what complaint you have to make against us which justifies you in attempting to destroy us and the State? In the first place did we not bring you into existence? Your father married your mother by our aid and begat you. Say whether you have any objection to urge against those of us who regulate marriage?

— None, I should reply.

— Or against those of us who regulate the system of nurture and education of children in which you were trained? Were not the laws, who have the charge of this, right in commanding your father to train you in music and gymnastic?

— Right, I should reply.

— Well, then, since you were brought into the world and nurtured and educated by us, can you deny in the first place that *you are our offspring and slave*, as your fathers were before you? And if this is true *you are not on equal terms with us*; nor can you think that you have a right to do to us what we are doing to you. Would you have any right to strike or revile or do any other evil to a father or to your master, if you had one, when you have been struck or reviled by him, or received some other evil at his hands?

— You would not say this? And because we think right to destroy you, do you think that you have any right to destroy us in return, and your country, as far as in you lies? And will you, O professor of true virtue, say that you are justified in this? Has a philosopher like you failed to discover that our country is more to be valued and higher and holier far than mother or father or any ancestor, and more to be regarded in the eyes of the gods and of men of understanding?

—Also to be soothed, and gently and reverently entreated when angry, even more than a father, and if not persuaded, obeyed? And when we are punished by her, whether with imprisonment or stripes, the punishment is to be endured in silence; and if she leads us to wounds or death in battle, thither we follow as is right; neither may anyone yield or retreat or leave his rank, *but whether in battle or in a court of law, or in any other place, he must do what his city and his country order him; or he must change their view of what is just*. And if he may do no violence to his father or mother, much less may he do violence to his country.

— What answer shall we make to this, Crito? Do the laws speak truly, or do they not?

*Cr*: I think that they do.

*Soc*: Then the laws will say:

— Consider, Socrates, if this is true, that in your present attempt you are going to do us wrong. For, after having brought you into the world, and nurtured and educated you, and given you and every other citizen a share in every good that we had to give, we further proclaim and give the right to every Athenian, that if he does not like us when he has come of age and has seen the ways of the city, and made our acquaintance, he may go where he pleases and take his goods with him; and none of us laws will forbid him or interfere with him. Any of you who does not like us and the city, and who wants to go to a colony or to any other city, may go where he likes, and take his goods with him. But he who has experience of the manner in which we order justice and administer the State, and still remains, has entered into an implied contract that he will do as we command him. And he who disobeys us is, as we maintain, thrice wrong: first, because in disobeying us he is disobeying his parents; secondly, because we are the authors of his education; thirdly, because he has made an agreement with us that he will duly obey our *commands*; and he neither obeys them *nor convinces us* that our commands are wrong; and we do not rudely impose them, but give him the alternative of obeying or *convincing us*; that is what we offer and he does neither. These are the sort of accusations to which, as we were saying, you, Socrates, will be exposed if you accomplish your intentions; you, above all other Athenians.

— Suppose I ask, why is this? they will justly retort upon me that I above all other men have acknowledged the agreement.

— There is clear proof, Socrates, that we and the city were not displeasing to you. Of all Athenians you have been the most constant resident in the city, which, as you never leave, you may be supposed to love. For you never went out of the city either to see the games, except once when you went to the Isthmus, or to any other place unless when you were on military service; nor did you travel as other men do. Nor had you any curiosity to know other States or their laws: your affections did not go beyond us and our State; we were your especial favorites, and you acquiesced in our government of you; and this is the State in which you begat your children, which is a proof of your satisfaction.

Moreover, you might, if you had liked, have fixed the penalty at banishment in the course of the trial. The State which refuses to let you go now would have let you go then. But you pretended that you preferred death to exile, and that you were not grieved at death. And now you have forgotten these fine sentiments, and pay no respect to us, the laws, of whom you are the destroyer; and *are doing what only a miserable slave would do*, running away and turning your back upon the compacts and agreements which you made as a citizen. And first of all answer this very question: Are we right in saying that you agreed to be governed according to us in deed, and not in word only? Is that true or not?

— How shall we answer that, Crito? Must we not agree?

*Cr*: There is no help, Socrates.

*Soc*: Then will they not say:

— You, Socrates, are breaking the covenants and agreements which you made with us at your leisure, not in any haste or under any compulsion or deception, but having had 70 years to think of them, during which time you were at liberty to leave the city, if we were not to your mind, or if our covenants appeared to you to be unfair. You had your choice, and might have gone either to Lacedaemon (Sparta) or Crete, which you often praise for their good government, or to some other Hellenic or foreign State. Whereas you, above all other Athenians, seemed to be so fond of the State, or, in other words, of us, her laws (for who would like a State that has no laws?), that you never stirred out of her... And now you run away and forsake your agreements. Not so, Socrates, if you will take our advice; do not make yourself ridiculous by escaping out of the city...

...Listen, then, Socrates, to us who have brought you up. Think not of life and children first, and of justice afterwards, but of justice first, that you may be justified before the princes of the world below. For neither will you nor any that belong to you be happier or holier or juster in this life, or happier in another, if you do as Crito bids.

*Now you depart in innocence, a sufferer and not a doer of evil; a victim, not of the laws, but of men.* But if you go forth, returning evil for evil, and injury for injury, breaking the covenants and agreements which you have made with us, and wronging those whom you ought least to wrong, that is to say, yourself, your friends, your country, and us, we shall be angry with you while you live, and *our brethren, the laws in the world below*, will receive you as an enemy; for they will know that you have done your best to destroy us. Listen, then, to us and not to Crito.

*Soc*: This is the voice which I seem to hear murmuring in my ears, like the sound of the flute in the ears of the mystic; that voice, I say, is humming in my ears, and prevents me from hearing any other. And I know that anything more which you will say will be in vain. Yet speak, if you have anything to say.

*Crito*: I have nothing to say, Socrates.

*Soc*: Then, Crito, let it be, and let us act in this way, since it is in this way that God leads us. (Plato, *Crito*, *50b*–54e.)

# 5

# LOVE WITHOUT DESIRE

## *Pederastic Love. Seducing Socrates. Diotima's Speech.*

*Love is the one thing that Socrates affirms he knows most about… There are at least two different words that differentiate erotic from non-erotic (filial) love. Eros, the god of love gives his name to the former, as does his mother Aphrodite, while 'philos' does duty for affection and friendship. Erotic relations become a model for philosophical intercourse not only because of the close nature of the teacher-taught relation; the word sunousia ('intercourse' literally: 'being together') is used for both. If desire is a basic fact of human existence, eros must be controlled, philosophically, by logos (reason). Both Socrates. and later Plato, find a way to redirect the erotic impulse into one of love, not of the body, but of the soul.*

*Although the body soul separation led to the distinction between a mortal body and an immortal soul, the latter idea may have been alien to Socrates, even as he devalued the cult of the body (so celebrated in Greek culture). Aristotle recalls Xenophon when he says that for Socrates corpses were useless and could be disposed of accordingly. In a culture where funeral rites and honours paid to the dead were important for both the family and the city, this cavalier attitude to mortal remains must have appeared shocking. The devaluation of the body at the expense of the psyche was the first step to the relocation of the virtues away from bodily vices.*

*Hence resistance to pleasure and pain, features which were marked as 'bodily' became a hall mark of the sage. Socrates was exceptional in this regard. If the real self is identified with the soul or psyche, the body can be viewed as its instrument. In Plato's* Alcibiades, *Socrates identifies the soul as the essence of man.*

*Socrates*: Is it an easy thing to know oneself, and was it a mere scamp who inscribed these words on the temple at Delphi; or is it a hard thing, not a task for anybody?

*Alcibiades*: I have often thought, Socrates, that it was easy for anybody; but often, too, that it was very hard.

*Soc*: But, Alcibiades, whether it is easy or not, here is the fact for us all the same: If we have that knowledge, we are likely to know what pains to take over ourselves; but if we have it not, we never can.

*Alc*: That is so.

*Soc*: You call talking and using speech the same thing, I suppose.

*Alc*: To be sure.

*Soc*: But the user and the thing he uses are different, are they not?

*Alc*: How do you mean?

*Soc*: For instance, I suppose a shoemaker uses a round tool, and a square one, and others, when he cuts.

*Alc*: Yes.

*Soc*: And the cutter and user is quite different from what he uses in cutting.

*Soc*: Well then, that is what I was asking just now — whether the user and what he uses are always, in your opinion, two different things.

*Alc*: They are.

*Soc*: Then what are we to say of the shoemaker? Does he cut with his tools only, or with his hands as well.

*Alc*: With his hands as well.

*Soc*: So he uses these also?

*Alc*: Yes.

*Soc*: Does he use his eyes, too, in his shoe-making?

*Alc*: Yes.

*Soc*: And we admit that the user and what he uses are different things?

*Alc*: Yes,

*Soc*: Then the shoemaker (is) different from the hands and eyes that (he uses)?

*Alc*: Apparently.

*Soc*: And man uses his whole body too?

*Alc*: To be sure.

*Soc*: So man is different from his own body?

*Alc*: It seems so.

*Soc*: Then what is man?

*Alc*: I cannot say.

*Soc*: Oh, but you can say that he is the user of the body.

*Alc*: Yes.

*Soc*: And the user of it must be the soul?

*Alc*: It must,

*Soc*: And ruler?

*Alc*: Yes.

*Soc*: ...Man must be one of three things.

*Alc*: What things?

*Soc*: Soul, body, or both together as one whole.

*Alc*: Very well.

*Soc*: But yet we have admitted that what actually rules the body is man?

*Alc*: We have.

*Soc*: And does the body rule itself ?

*Alc*: By no means.

*Soc*: Then that cannot be what we are seeking.

*Alc*: It seems not.

*Soc*: Well then, does the combination of the two rule the body, so that we are to regard this as man?

*Alc*: Perhaps it is.

*Soc*: The unlikeliest thing in the world: For if one of the two does not share in the rule, it is quite inconceivable that the combination of the two can be ruling.

*Alc*: You are right.

*Soc*: But since neither the body nor the combination of the two is man, we are reduced, I suppose, to this: Either man is nothing at all, or if something, he turns out to be nothing else than soul.

*Alc*: Precisely so.

*Soc*: Well, do you require some yet clearer proof that the soul is man.

*Alc*: No, I assure you: I think it is amply proved (Plato, *Alcibiades–1*, 128–130)

## Pederastic Love

*Ancient Greek society had different sexual mores from later norms. Sexual relations between males was not entirely frowned upon. There were in fact complex rules that socially governed the conduct of the older active male (the erastes or lover) and the youth (the passive eromenos) he was erotically attracted to. The Greeks had no word like homosexual (a much later conception). Their term was pederasty (the love of boys). Socrates's engagement with beautiful boys, based on a distinction between body and soul, was spiritual, not physical. The soul (or what we might call the personality) became the object of love. Xenophon recalls Socrates replacing sensuality with sensibility, valuing self-control over all else.*

Of sensual passion he would say: Avoid it resolutely. It is not easy to control yourself once you meddle with that sort of thing. Thus, on hearing that Critobulus had kissed Alcibiades's pretty boy, he put this question to Xenophon before Critobulus.

*Socrates*: Tell me, Xenophon, did you not suppose Critobulus to be a sober person, and by no means rash; prudent, and not thoughtless or adventurous?

— Certainly, said Xenophon.

— Then you are to look on him henceforth as utterly hot-headed and reckless. The man would do a somersault into a ring of knives; he would jump into fire.

— What on earth has he done to make you think so badly of him? asked Xenophon.

— What has the man done? He dared to kiss Alcibiades's son, and the boy is very good-looking and attractive.

— Oh, if that is the sort of adventure you mean, I think I might make that venture myself.

— Poor fellow! What do you think will happen to you through kissing a pretty face?

Won't you lose your liberty in a trice and become a slave, begin spending large sums on harmful pleasures, have no time to give to anything fit for a gentleman, be forced to concern yourself with things that no madman even would care about?

— Heracles! what alarming power in a kiss! cried Xenophon.

— What? Does that surprise you? continued Socrates, Don't you know that the scorpion, though smaller than an obol, if it but fasten on the tongue, inflicts excruciating and maddening pain?

— Yes, to be sure; for the scorpion injects something by its bite.

— And do you think, you foolish fellow, that the fair inject nothing when they kiss, just because you don't see it? Don't you know that this creature called 'fair and young' is more dangerous than the scorpion, seeing that it need not even come in contact, like the insect, but at any distance can inject a maddening poison into anyone who only looks at it?

...Thus in the matter of carnal appetite, he held that those whose passions were not under complete control should limit themselves to such indulgence as the soul would reject unless the need of the body were pressing, and such as would do no harm when the need was there. As for his own conduct in this matter, it was evident that he had trained himself to avoid the fairest and most attractive more easily than others avoid the ugliest and most repulsive. Concerning eating and drinking then and carnal indulgence such were his views, and he thought that a due portion of pleasure would be no more lacking to him than to those who give themselves much to these, and that much less trouble would fall to his lot. (Xenophon, *Memorabilia*, 1.3.8–15.)

*Xenophon also wrote a* Symposium, *dated to a couple of years after Aristophanes's* Clouds *(to which it refers). Unlike the formally structured and better known dialogue of Plato's, Xenophon's work is more freewheeling, moving from subject to subject.*

*While Socrates agrees that pederasty is superior to heterosexual love, he aims to detach it from its physical aspect to a spiritual relation (this is really what 'Platonic love' means). By separating the soul from the body as the proper object of desire, Socrates is indirectly describing his own relations with the young men whom he spends time with. He also adduces reasons why such sublimated desire is preferable to the pursuit of purely bodily pleasures.*

*Socrates*: Gentlemen, it is to be expected of us, is it not, when in the presence of a mighty deity that is coeval with the eternal gods, yet youngest of them all in appearance, in magnitude encompassing the universe, but enthroned in the heart of man, I mean Love, that we should not be unmindful of him, particularly in view of the fact that we are all of his following?

...Now, whether there is one Aphrodite or two, 'Heavenly' and 'Vulgar,' I do not know for even Zeus, though considered one and the same, yet has many bynames. I do know, however, that in the case of Aphrodite there are separate altars and temples for the two, and also rituals, those of the 'Vulgar' Aphrodite excelling in looseness, those of the 'heavenly' in chastity. One might conjecture, also, that different types of love come from the different sources, carnal love from the 'Vulgar Aphrodite', and from the 'Heavenly' spiritual love, love of friendship and of noble conduct. That is the sort of love, Callias, that seems to have you in its grip. I infer this from the noble nature of the one you love and because I see that you include his father in your meetings with him. For the virtuous lover does not make any of these matters a secret from the father of his beloved.

— Marry, quoth Hermogenes, you arouse my admiration in numerous ways, Socrates, but now more than ever, because in the very act of flattering Callias you are in fact educating him to conform to the ideal.

— True, he replied; and to add to his pleasure, I wish to bear testimony to him that spiritual love is far superior to carnal. (Xenophon, *Symposium*, 8.12.)

## Seducing Socrates

*Plato's* Symposium, *a dialogue of his middle period (more Platonic than Socratic), nevertheless touches on several different aspects of the personality of Socrates. The dialogue celebrates Aristocratic post dinner drinking parties (replacing songs and music with philosophical speeches). The subject proposed on this occasion is love.*

*Different people, including Aristophanes, the author of the* Clouds, *offer accounts of the nature of love. Alcibiades arrives, drunk, after all the speeches have been made.*

*Urged, he chooses to speak about Socrates (the first part, Socrates as a satyr has been quoted earlier). Here he gives a report of his attempt to seduce Socrates. We must note that despite the dramatic immediacy of the passage, it was written long after both the characters had passed away.*

*Alcibiades*: Now I fancied that he was seriously enamoured of my beauty, and I thought that I should therefore have a grand opportunity of hearing him tell what he knew, for I had a wonderful opinion of the attractions of my youth. In the prosecution of this design, when I next went to him, I sent away the attendant who usually accompanied me (I will confess the whole truth, and beg you to listen; and if I speak falsely, do you, Socrates, expose the falsehood). Well, he and I were alone together, and I thought that when there was nobody with us, I should hear him speak the language which lovers use to their loves when they are by themselves, and I was delighted. Nothing of the sort; he conversed as usual, and spent the day with me and then went away.

Afterwards I challenged him to the palaestra; and he wrestled and closed with me several times when there was no one present; I fancied that I might succeed in this manner. Not a bit; I made no way with him. Lastly, as I had failed hitherto, I thought that I must take stronger measures and attack him boldly, and, as I had begun, not give him up, but see how matters stood between him and me. So I invited him to sup with me, just as if he were a fair youth, and I a designing lover. He was not easily persuaded to come; he did, however, after a while accept the invitation, and when he came the first time, he wanted to go away at once as soon as supper was over, and I had not the face to detain him.

The second time, still in pursuance of my design, after we had supped, I went on conversing far into the night, and when he wanted to go away, I pretended that the hour was late and that he had much better remain. So he lay down on the couch next to me, the same on which he had supped, and there was no one but ourselves sleeping in the apartment. All this may be told without shame to any one. But what follows I could hardly tell you if I were sober…

When the lamp was put out and the servants had gone away, I thought that I must be plain with him and have no more ambiguity. So I gave him a shake, and I said:

'Socrates, are you asleep?' 'No,' he said. 'Do you know what I am meditating?' 'What are you meditating?' he said. 'I think,' I replied, 'that of all the lovers whom I have ever had you are the only one who is worthy of me, and you appear to be too modest to speak. Now I feel that I should be a fool to refuse you this or any other favour, and therefore I come to lay at your feet all that I have and all that my friends have, in the hope that you will assist me in the way of virtue, which I desire above all things, and in which I believe that you can help me better than anyone else. And I should certainly have more reason to be ashamed of what wise men would say if I were to refuse a favour to such as you, than of what the world, who are mostly fools, would say of me if I granted it.'

To these words he replied in the ironical manner which is so characteristic of him:

— Alcibiades, my friend, you have indeed an elevated aim if what you say is true, and if there really is in me any power by which you may become better; truly you must see in me some rare beauty of a kind infinitely higher than any which I see in you. And therefore, if you mean to share with me and to exchange beauty for beauty, you will have greatly the advantage of me; you will gain true beauty in return for appearance — gold in exchange for brass...

Whereupon, I fancied that he was smitten, and that the words which I had uttered like arrows had wounded him, and so without waiting to hear more I got up, and throwing my coat about him crept under his threadbare cloak, as the time of year was winter, and there I lay during the whole night having this wonderful monster in my arms. This again, Socrates, will not be denied by you. And yet, notwithstanding all, he was so superior to my solicitations, so contemptuous and derisive and disdainful of my beauty — which really, as I fancied, had some attractions — hear, O judges; for judges you shall be of the haughty virtue of Socrates — nothing more happened, but in the morning when I awoke (let all the gods and goddesses be my witnesses) I arose as from the couch of a father or an elder brother (Plato, *Symposium*, 217d–218d, trans. B. Jowett)

## Diotima's Speech

*Socratic resistance to the advances of Alcibiades mimics in some respects the active/passive role that the lover and beloved play in the standard Greek account of pederasty. But the older Socrates, who should have been the seducer resists the advances of the younger and so more desirable Alcibiades.*

*In the Symposium, Socrates speaks as well, claiming he is repeating, what a wise woman (perhaps a mantic or seer), once told him. The nature of eros (the boy-god of love) is, as the speech unfolds, reminiscent of Socrates himself. Plato lets Socrates, through the voice of a woman, draw a portrait of Socrates and philosophy. The choice of a woman, given the standard Greek attitude towards women, is itself remarkable. Plato has here feminized male erotic discourse, introducing the idea of reciprocal desire and merging the language of sexual pleasure with the reproductive function of women. The metaphor of male pregnancy — a condition and not a consequence of erotic intercourse, leads to the birth of ideas rather than children, picking up the theme of immortality that runs through the dialogue. I highlight some key sections, which echo what has been said of Socrates elsewhere: his poverty, his asceticism, his lack of knowledge, or ignorance, which is not absolute, for he is aware of it, as necessary in a pursuit of wisdom. He too, like eros, is midway between what he lacks and what he desires. The aim of love, we are told, is the good, which recalls the Socratic claim that all men desire the good (or beneficial). The later part of the speech, the ascent from visible to invisible forms of beauty is seen as a poetic expression of Plato's own theory of forms, moving from particular instances to the abstract conception of Beauty.*

I would rehearse a tale of love which I heard from Diotima of Mantineia, a woman wise in this and in many other kinds of knowledge, who in the days of old, when the Athenians offered sacrifice before the coming of the plague, delayed the disease by 10 years. She was my instructress in the art of love, and I shall repeat to you what she said to me... and I shall take both parts myself as well as I can. As you, Agathon, suggested, I must speak first of the being and nature of Love, and then of his works.

First I said to her... that Love was a mighty god, and likewise fair; and she proved to me that, by my own showing, Love was neither fair nor good.

— What do you mean, Diotima, I said, is love then evil and foul?

— Hush, she cried; must that be foul which is not fair?

— Certainly, I said.

— And is that which is not wise, ignorant? do you not see that there is a mean between wisdom and ignorance?

— And what may that be? I said.

— 'Right opinion', she replied; which, as you know, being incapable of giving a reason, is not knowledge (for how can knowledge be devoid of reason? nor again, ignorance, for neither can ignorance attain the truth), but is clearly something which is a mean between ignorance and wisdom.

— Quite true, I replied.

— Do not then insist, she said, that what is not fair is of necessity foul, or what is not good evil; or infer that because love is not fair and good he is therefore foul and evil; for he is in a mean between them.

— Well, I said, Love is surely admitted by all to be a great god.

— By those who know or by those who do not know?

— By all.

— And how, Socrates, she said with a smile, can Love be acknowledged to be a great god by those who say that he is not a god at all?

— And who are they? I said.

— You and I are two of them, she replied.

— How can that be?

— It is quite intelligible, she replied; for you yourself would acknowledge that the gods are happy and fair — of course you would — would you dare to say that any god was not?

— Certainly not, I replied.

— And you mean by the happy, those who are the possessors of things good or fair?

— Yes, and you admitted that Love, because he was in want, desires those good and fair things of which he is in want?

— Yes, I did. But how can he be a god who has no portion in what is either good or fair?

— Impossible.

— Then you see that you also deny the divinity of Love.

— What then is Love? I asked; Is he mortal?

— No... As in the former instance, he is neither mortal nor immortal, but in a mean between the two.

— What is he, Diotima?

— He is a great spirit (daimon), and like all spirits he is intermediate between the divine and the mortal.

— And what, I said, is his power?

— He interprets, she replied, between gods and men, conveying and taking across to the gods the prayers and sacrifices of men and to men the commands and replies of the gods; he is the mediator who spans the chasm which divides them, and therefore in him all is bound together, and through him the arts of the prophet and the priest, their sacrifices and mysteries and charms, and all prophecy and incantation, find their way. For God mingles not with man; but through Love all the intercourse and converse of God with man, whether awake or asleep, is carried on. The wisdom which understands this is spiritual; all other wisdom, such as that of arts and handicrafts, is mean and vulgar. Now these spirits or intermediate powers are many and diverse, and one of them is Love.

— And who, I said, was his father, and who his mother?

— The tale, she said, will take time; nevertheless I will tell you. On the birthday of Aphrodite there was a feast of the gods, at which the god Poros or Plenty, who is the son of Metis or Discretion, was one of the guests. When the feast was over, Penia or Poverty, as the manner is on such occasions, came about the doors to beg. Now Plenty who was the worse for nectar (there was no wine in those days), went into the garden of Zeus and fell into a heavy sleep, and Poverty considering her own straitened circumstances, plotted to have a child by him, and accordingly she lay down at his side and conceived Love, who partly because he is naturally a lover of the beautiful, and because Aphrodite is herself beautiful, and also because he was born on her birthday, is her follower, and attendant. And as his parentage is, so also are his fortunes. In the first place *he is always poor,* and *anything but tender and fair*, as the many imagine him; and *he is rough and squalid*, and *has no shoes,* nor a house to dwell in; on the bare earth exposed he lies under the open heaven, in the streets, or at the doors of houses, taking his rest; and like his mother he is always in distress. Like his father too, whom he also partly resembles, he is always plotting against the fair and good; *he is bold, enterprising, strong, a mighty hunter*, always weaving some intrigue or other, *keen in the pursuit of wisdom*, fertile in resources; *a philosopher at all times*, terrible as an *enchanter, sorcerer, sophist*. He is by nature neither mortal nor immortal, but alive and flourishing at one moment when he is in plenty, and dead at another moment, and again alive by reason of his fathers nature. But that which is always flowing in is always flowing out, and so he is never in want and never in wealth; and, further, he is *in a mean between ignorance and knowledge*. The truth of the matter is this: No god is a philosopher or seeker after wisdom, for he is wise already; nor does any man who is wise seek after wisdom. Neither do the ignorant seek after wisdom. For herein is the evil of ignorance, that he who is neither good nor wise is nevertheless satisfied with himself. He has no desire for that of which he feels no want.

— But who then, Diotima, I said, are the lovers of wisdom, if they are neither the wise nor the foolish?

— A child may answer that question, she replied; they are those who are in a mean between the two; Love is one of them. For wisdom is a most beautiful thing, and Love is of the beautiful; and therefore *Love is also a philosopher or lover of wisdom*, and being a lover of wisdom is in a mean between the wise and the ignorant.

And of this too his birth is the cause; for his father is wealthy and wise, and his mother poor and foolish. Such, my dear Socrates, is the nature of the spirit Love. The error in your conception of him was very natural, and as I imagine from what you say, has arisen out of a confusion of love and the beloved, which made you think that love was all beautiful. For the beloved is the truly beautiful, and delicate, and perfect, and blessed; but the principle of love is of another nature, and is as I have described.

— I said, O thou stranger woman, thou sayest well; but, assuming Love to be such as you say, what is the use of him to men?

— That, Socrates, she replied, I will attempt to unfold: Of his nature and birth I have already spoken; and you acknowledge that love is of the beautiful. But someone will say: Of the beautiful in what, Socrates and Diotima — or rather let me put the question more clearly, and ask: When a man loves the beautiful, what does he desire?

— I answered her: That the beautiful may be his.

— Still, she said, the answer suggests a further question: What is given by the possession of beauty?

— To what you have asked, I replied, I have no answer ready.

— Then, she said, let me put the word 'good' in the place of the beautiful, and repeat the question once more: If he who loves loves the good, what is it then that he loves?

— *The possession of the good*, I said.

— *And what does he gain who possesses the good?*

— *Happiness*, I replied; there is less difficulty in answering that question.

— Yes, she said, the happy are made happy by the acquisition of good things.

Nor is there any need to ask why a man desires happiness; the answer is already final. And is this wish and this desire common to all? And do all *men always desire their own good*, or only some men?

— All men, I replied; the desire is common to all.

— Why, then, she rejoined, are not all men, Socrates, said to love, but only some of them? Whereas you say that all men are always loving the same things.

— I myself wonder, I said, why this is.

— There is nothing to wonder at, she replied; the reason is that one part of love is separated off and receives the name of the whole, but the other parts have other names.

— Give an illustration, I said.

She answered me as follows: There is poetry, which, as you know, is complex and manifold. All creation or passage of non-being into being is poetry or making, and the processes of all art are creative; and the masters of arts are all poets or makers. Very true. Still, she said, you know that they are not called poets, but have other names; only that portion of the art which is separated off from the rest, and is concerned with music and metre, is termed poetry, and they who possess poetry in this sense of the word are called poets.

— And the same holds of love.

*For you may say generally that all desire of good and happiness is only the great and subtle power of love; but they who are drawn towards him by any other path, whether the path of money-making or gymnastics or philosophy, are not called lovers — the name of the whole is appropriated to those whose affection takes one form only — they alone are said to love, or to be lovers.*

— I dare say, I replied, that you are right.

— Yes, she added, and you hear people say that lovers are seeking their other half; but I say that they are seeking neither the half of themselves, nor the whole, unless the half or the whole be also a good. And they will cut off their own hands and feet and cast them away, if they are evil; for they love not what is their own, unless perchance there be some one who calls what belongs to him the good, and what belongs to another the evil. For there is nothing which men love but the good... Then love, she said, may be described generally as the love of the everlasting possession of the good?

— That is most true.

— Then if this be the nature of love, can you tell me further, she said, what is the manner of the pursuit? What are they doing who show all this eagerness and heat which is called love? And what is the object which they have in view? Answer me.

*Diotima*: I mean to say, that all men are bringing to the birth in their bodies and in their souls. There is a certain age at which human nature is desirous of procreation — procreation which must be in beauty and not in deformity; and this procreation is the union of man and woman, and is a divine thing; for conception and generation are an immortal principle in the mortal creature, and in the inharmonious they can never be.

...To the mortal creature, generation is a sort of eternity and immortality... and if, as has been already admitted, love is of the everlasting possession of the good, all men will necessarily desire immortality together with good: Wherefore love is of immortality.

*Socrates*: All this she taught me at various times when she spoke of love. And I remember her once saying to me...

— Think only of the ambition of men, and you will wonder at the senselessness of their ways, unless you consider how they are stirred by the love of an immortality of fame. They are ready to run all risks greater far than they would have to run for their children, and to spend money and undergo any sort of toil, and even to die, for the sake of leaving behind them a name which shall be eternal... Those who are pregnant in the body only, betake themselves to women and beget children — this is the character of their love; their offspring, as they hope, will preserve their memory and giving them the blessedness and immortality which they desire in the future. But *souls which are pregnant — for there certainly are men who are more creative in their souls than in their bodies — conceive that which is proper for the soul to conceive or contain. And what are these conceptions? Wisdom and virtue in general.* And such creators are poets and all artists who are deserving of the name inventor. But the greatest and fairest sort of wisdom by far is that which is concerned with the ordering of states and families, and which is called temperance and justice.

— These are the lesser mysteries of love, into which even you, Socrates, may enter; to the greater and more hidden ones which are the crown of these, and to which, if you pursue them in a right spirit, they will lead, I know not whether you will be able to attain.

— He who has been instructed thus far in the things of love, and who has learned to see the beautiful in due order and succession, when he comes toward the end will suddenly perceive a nature of wondrous beauty (and this, Socrates, is the final cause of all our former toils)... Remember how in that communion only, beholding beauty with the eye of the mind, he will be enabled to bring forth, not images of beauty, but realities (for he has hold not of an image but of a reality), and bringing forth and nourishing true virtue to become the friend of God and be immortal, if mortal man may, would that be an ignoble life?

Such, Phaedrus — and I speak not only to you, but to all of you — were the words of Diotima; and I am persuaded of their truth. *And being persuaded of them, I try to persuade others,* that in the attainment of this end human nature will not easily find a helper better than love. (Plato, *Symposium*, 201d–210a.)

# 6

# THE EXAMINED LIFE

## *Socratic Dialogue. Contra Rhetoric. The Elenchus.*

*For Socrates dialogue or conversation was the way to practice philosophy. Consistent with his claim not to know, he taught not by instruction but by interrogation. Those writers who memorialized him recalled these conversations. Socratic literature is a written record of what he is supposed to have said, and a memory of what he had done. The dialogue form enabled those who did write, to put into direct discourse what they recalled of his words. There is general agreement about the nature of these conversations, mainly concerned with morality, with right conduct or, to use the term that encapsulated it, with justice. Socrates went about asking questions about moral issues rather than telling people how they ought to behave. Aristotle confirms this, adding that*

*Socrates did not give any answers since he claimed he didn't know. These were not random questions but had to do with how best to conduct oneself. Through a quasi-judicial mode of interrogation, Socrates examined the beliefs of his fellow citizens, with the aim of directing them to examine their own beliefs. The fact that the questioning did not lead to any positive result was not the failure of the method, but underscored the importance of the process: The need for questioning and examining central moral beliefs. This is what Socrates means when he asserted that the unexamined life is not worth living. The Socratic examination, as we have seen, was life changing for those who he came into contact with. It also annoyed those who were shown to know less than they claimed to.*

## Socratic Dialogue

*Socrates*: So I proceeded to say — Protagoras, do not suppose that I have any other desire in debating with you than to examine the difficulties which occur to myself at each point. For I hold that there is good deal in what Homer says 'When two go together, one observes before the other' for somehow it makes all of us human beings more resourceful in every deed or word or thought; but if one observes something alone, forthwith one has to go about searching until one discovers somebody to whom one can show it off and who can corroborate it. (Plato, *Protagoras*, 348c.)

*Thrasymachus*: What is all this nonsense, Socrates? Why do you go on in this childish way being so polite about each other's opinions? If you really want to know what justice is, stop asking questions and then playing to the gallery by refuting anyone who answers you. You know...it is easier to ask questions than to answer them. Give us an answer yourself and tell us what justice is... Give me a clear and precise definition. (Plato, *Republic*, 336c–d.)

*Socrates is remembered as a potent speaker: He upset arguments and those who made them. Socrates, at his trial, denies being an orator at all, but this is a standard rhetorical ploy; a good speaker often claims not to be clever, and so truthful. Xenophon says otherwise:*

Socrates was clever in rhetorical matters, as Idomeneus also says: And the Thirty forbade him from teaching technical rhetoric. And Aristophanes satirizes him as someone who makes the weaker argument stronger. And indeed he was the first, along with his pupil Aeschines, to teach rhetoric. (Xenophon, *Memorablia*, 1.31.)

*At his trial Socrates denies that he is a clever speaker and so, deceitful.*

*Socrates: Of the many lies they told, one in particular surprised me, namely that you should be careful not to be deceived by an accomplished speaker like me. That they were not ashamed to be immediately proved wrong by the facts, when I show myself not to be an accomplished speaker at all, that I thought was most shameless on their part — unless indeed they call an accomplished speaker the man who speaks the truth. If they mean that, I would agree that I am an orator, but not after their manner, for indeed, as as I say, practically nothing they said was true. (Plato, Apology, 17a–c.)*

## Contra Rhetoric

*Plato is careful to distinguish Socrates from the sophists who offered to teach the art of debate or rhetoric for a fee. Socratic dialogue as we have seen from excerpts, never teaches, only assists in examination. Socrates did not take any money from his associates. In conversation with the well known rhetorician Gorgias (Plato names the dialogue after him), and his pupil, Polus (the name means a colt, or an unbridled horse, much like the character), Socrates tells us what he thinks rhetoric is.*

*Socrates*: Ah, sweet Polus, of course it is for this very purpose we possess ourselves of companions and sons, that when the advance of years begins to make us stumble, you younger ones may be at hand *to set our lives upright again in words as well as deeds*. So now if Gorgias and I are stumbling in our words, you are to stand by and set us up again — it is only your duty; and for my part I am willing to revoke at your pleasure anything that you think has been wrongly admitted, if you will kindly observe one condition.

*Polus*: What do you mean by that?

*Soc*: That you keep a check on that lengthy way of speaking, Polus, which you tried to employ at first.

*Polus*: Why, shall I not be at liberty to say as much as I like?

*Soc*: It would indeed be a hard fate for you, my excellent friend, if having come to Athens, where there is more freedom of speech than anywhere in Greece, you should be the one person there who could not enjoy it. But as a set-off to that, I ask you if it would not be just as hard on me, while you spoke at length and refused to answer my questions, not to be free to go away and avoid listening to you. No, if you have any concern for the argument that we have carried on, and care to set it on its feet again, revoke whatever you please, as I suggested just now; take your turn in questioning and being questioned... And thus either refute or be refuted.

*Polus*: So answer me this, Socrates, since you think that Gorgias is at a loss about rhetoric, what is your own account of it?

*Soc*: Are you asking what art (branch of knowledge) I call it?

*Polus*: Yes.

*Soc*: None at all, I consider it, Polus, if you would have the honest truth, a certain habitude.

*Polus*: Then do you take rhetoric to be a habitude? Habitude of what?

*Soc*: Of producing a kind of gratification and pleasure.

*Polus*: Then you take rhetoric to be something fine — an ability to gratify people?

*Soc*: How now, Polus? Have you as yet heard me tell you what I say it is, that you ask what should follow that — whether I do not take it to be fine?

*Polus*: Why, did I not hear you call it a certain habitude?

*Soc*: Then please — since you value ‹gratification' — be so good as gratify me in a small matter... Ask me now what art I take cookery to be.

*Polus*: Then I ask you, what art is cookery?

*Soc*: None at all, Polus.

*Polus*: Then what is it?

*Soc*: I reply, a certain habitude.

*Polus*: Of what? Tell me.

*Soc*: Of production of gratification and pleasure, Polus.

*Polus*: So cookery and rhetoric are the same thing?

*Soc*: Not at all, only parts of the same practice.

*Polus*: What practice do you mean?

*Soc*: I fear it may be too rude to tell the truth; for I shrink from saying it on Gorgias's account, lest he suppose I am making satirical fun of his own profession... What I call rhetoric is a part of a certain business which has nothing fine about it.

*Gorgias*: What is that, Socrates? Tell us, without scruple on my account.

*Soc*: It seems to me then, Gorgias, to be a pursuit that is not a matter of art, but showing a shrewd, gallant spirit which has a natural bent for clever dealing with mankind, and I sum up its substance in the name flattery. (Plato, *Gorgias*, 461d–463a)

*According to Socrates, rhetoric persuades because it flatters; it teaches speakers to say what the audience wants to hear. Demagogues use rhetorical skills to persuade the masses. Unlike dialectic it does not aim at truth or engage with questions of morality. Xenophon reports a conversation with the polymath, Hippias:*

In his conversations with different persons; I recollect the substance of one that he had with Hippias of Elis concerning Justice. Hippias, who had not been in Athens for a considerable time, found Socrates talking: He was saying that if you want to have a man taught cobbling or building or smithing or riding, you know where to send him to learn the craft; some indeed declare that if you want to train up a horse or an ox in the way he should go, teachers abound. And yet, strangely enough, if you want to learn Justice yourself, or to have your son or servant taught it, you know not where to go for a teacher.

When Hippias heard this: 'How now?' he cried, in a tone of raillery, 'Still the same old sentiments, Socrates, that I heard from you so long ago?'

— Yes, Hippias, Socrates replied, always the same, and what is more astonishing on the same topics too! You are so learned that I daresay you never say the same thing on the same subjects.

— I certainly try to say something fresh every time.

— Do you mean, about what you know? For example, in answer to the question,

'How many letters are there in Socrates and how do you spell it? Do you try to say something different now from what you said before? Or take figures: Suppose you are asked if twice five are ten, don't you give the same answer now as you gave before?

— About letters and figures, Socrates, I always say the same thing, just like you. As for Justice, I feel confident that I can now say that which neither you nor anyone else can contradict... But I vow you shall not hear unless you first declare your own opinion about the nature of Justice; for it's enough that you mock at others, questioning and examining everybody, and never willing to render an account yourself or to state an opinion about anything. (Xenophon, *Memorablia*, IV.6.13–15.)

*Although Socratic examination revealed the ignorance of those who thought they knew, it had the result of making them aware of their lack of knowledge and hence was an educational tool. One positive way of seeing this is noted by Plato in a late dialogue, the Sophist.*

*Socrates*: Of instruction in arguments one method seems to be rougher, and the other smoother.

*Theaetetus*: What shall we call each of these?

*Soc*: The venerable method of our fathers, which they generally employed towards their sons, and which many still employ, of sometimes showing anger at their errors and sometimes more gently exhorting them — that would most properly be called as a whole admonition.

*Tht*: That is true.

*Soc*: On the other hand, some appear to have convinced themselves that all ignorance is involuntary, and that he who thinks himself wise would never be willing to learn any of those things in which he believes he is clever, and that the admonition kind of education takes a deal of trouble and accomplishes little.

*Tht*: They are quite right.

*Soc*: So they set themselves to cast out the conceit of cleverness in another way.

*Tht*: In what way?

*Soc*: They question a man about the things which he thinks he is talking sense when he is talking nonsense; then they easily discover that his opinions are like those of men who wander, and in their discussions they collect those opinions and compare them with one another, and by the comparison they show that they contradict one another about the same things, in relation to the same things and in respect to the same things. But those who see this grow angry with themselves and gentle towards others, and this is the way in which they are freed from their high and obstinate opinions about themselves. The process of freeing them, moreover, affords the greatest pleasure to the listeners and the most lasting benefit to him who is subjected to it. For just as physicians who care for the body believe that the body cannot benefit from any food offered to it until all obstructions are removed, so, my boy, those who purge the soul believe that the soul can receive no benefit from any teachings offered to it until someone by cross-questioning (*elenchôn*) reduces him who is cross-questioned (*elenchomenon*) to an attitude of modesty, by removing the opinions that obstruct the teachings, and thus purges him and makes him think that he knows only what he knows, and no more... For all these reasons, Theaetetus, we must assert that cross-questioning is the greatest and most efficacious of all purifications, and that he who is not cross-questioned, even though he be the Great King (the Persian monarch), has not been purified of the greatest taints, and is therefore uneducated and deformed in those things in which he who is to be truly happy ought to be most pure and beautiful. (Plato, *Sophist*, 230b–c.)

*Socrates questioned the moral beliefs of others by asking them the meaning of key moral terms. His search for definitions aimed at discovering some common characteristic that covered all instances to which the term applied. This demand was not always clearly understood by his contemporaries. In Plato's* Meno *Socrates asks for a definition of virtue:*

*Socrates*: Do tell me, in heaven's name, what is your own account of virtue.

Speak out frankly, that I may find myself the victim of a most fortunate falsehood, if you prove to have knowledge of it, while I have said that I never yet came across anyone who had.

*Meno*: Why, there is no difficulty, Socrates. First of all, if you take the virtue of a man, it is easily stated that a man's virtue is this — that he be competent to manage the affairs of his city, and to manage them *so as to benefit his friends and harm his enemies, and to take care to avoid suffering harm himself*. Or take a woman's virtue: There is no difficulty in describing it as the duty of ordering the house well, looking after the property indoors, and obeying her husband. And the child has another virtue — one for the female, and one for the male; and there is another for elderly men — one, if you like, for freemen, and yet another for slaves. And there are very many other virtues besides, so that one cannot be at a loss to explain what virtue is; for it is according to each activity and age that every one of us, in whatever we do, has his virtue; and the same, I take it, Socrates, will hold also of vice.

*Soc*: I seem to be in a most lucky way, Meno; for in seeking one virtue I have discovered a whole swarm of virtues there in your keeping. Now, Meno, to follow this figure of a swarm, suppose I should ask you what is the real nature of the bee, and you replied that there are many different kinds of bees, and I rejoined: Do you say it is by being bees that they are of many and various kinds and differ from each other, or does their difference lie not in that, but in something else — for example, in their beauty or size or some other quality? Tell me, what would be your answer to this question?

*Meno*: Why, this — that they do not differ, as bees, the one from the other.

*Soc*: And if I went on to say: What do you call the quality by which they do not differ, but are all alike? You could find me an answer, I presume?

*Meno*: I could.

*Soc*: And likewise also with the virtues, however many and various they may be, they *all have one common character* whereby they are virtues, and on which one would of course be wise to keep an eye when one is giving a definitive answer to the question of what virtue really is. You take my meaning, do you not?

*Meno*: My impression is that I do; but still I do not yet grasp the meaning of the question as I could wish.

*Soc*: Is it only in the case of virtue, do you think, Meno, that one can say there is one kind belonging to a man, another to a woman, and so on with the rest, or is it just the same, too, in the case of health and size and strength? Do you consider that there is one health for a man, and another for a woman? Or, wherever we find health, is it of the same character universally, in a man or in anyone else?

*Meno*: I think that health is the same, both in man and in woman.

> *Soc: Then is it not so with size and strength also. If a woman is strong, she will be strong by reason of the same form and the same strength; by 'the same' I mean that strength does not differ as strength, whether it be in a man or in a woman. Or do you think there is any difference?*
> *Meno: I do not.*
> *Soc: And will virtue, as virtue, differ at all whether it be in a child or in an elderly person, in a woman or in a man? (Plato, Meno, 72a–73b.)*

## The Elenchus

*Socrates did not ask random questions. In Plato's early dialogues his questions, centred on moral concepts, are methodically employed. The 'examination' that Socrates undertook was quasi-judicial. His instrument was the elenchus; the noun is derived from a verb meaning 'to examine' or 'to cross examine'. The person he questions, the respondent, initially offers something like a definition of a concept. Often he is wide off the mark — producing, as Meno did, an instance or example of what is sought rather than its 'essential feature'. Through further examination, Socrates shows that the offered definition contradicts other beliefs the respondent holds. The initial definition may then be either abandoned or modified. The examination goes on. Usually the discussion ends in an impasse or aporia (difficulty). In Plato's account, the Elenchus is the central method of Socratic examination, bringing out the beliefs of those whom he questions and demonstrating to them that what they thought they knew, they actually were confused about.*

*The inquiry is limited to beliefs the respondent himself holds. Socrates will not examine second hand beliefs, attributed to others not present. This is an important condition and regularly insisted on, because the force of the Socratic method lies in its ability to confront a person with his own ignorance, thus getting him to abandon his false beliefs. It emphasizes the importance of philosophy as an active exercise of reason, rather than merely an academic pursuit, or a purely intellectual exercise meant to sharpen the intellect of young men before they move on to civic and political careers. Philosophy as a discipline is both protreptic and transformative. This limitation also rules out the acceptance of received wisdom. Truth is not to be found in some religious, political or poetic authority. If the respondent does not agree to a step in the examination, the argument cannot proceed.*

*The Elenchus has mainly a negative function: It can disprove a thesis, but not prove one directly. It is aligned with Socrates's claim not to know. At best, like the reductio, it provides an indirect proof for a thesis by showing that its denial leads to a contradiction: that the respondent holds inconsistent beliefs. Since Socrates cannot give us any positive beliefs of his own, he is apparently unable to argue for any real moral thesis.*

*But he believes that ethics is objective; moral concepts are not conventionally variable, as some of the Sophists claimed. In the debate between nature (phusis) and culture (nomos), Socrates held that moral truths are given, invariable and must be discovered.*

*Socratic questioning can lead to paradoxical conclusions, as the respondent is forced to admit something he finds difficult if not impossible to accept. The search for a definition of justice creates confusion among the speakers in the first book of* the Republic. *A series of definitions of justice are offered, but are turned upside down. Here Socrates is in conversation with Polemarchus who cites the poet Simonides in the somewhat standard formulation of justice as a kind of reciprocity.*

*Socrates*: Tell me, then, what it is that you affirm that Simonides says and rightly says about justice.

*Polemarchus*: That it is just to render to each his due. In saying this I think he speaks well.

— I must admit, said I (*Socrates narrates the entire dialogue*), that it is not easy to disbelieve Simonides. For he is a wise and inspired man. But just what he may mean by this, you, Polemarchus, doubtless know, but I do not. Obviously he does not mean what we were just speaking of, this return of a deposit to anyone whatsoever even if he asks it back when not in his right mind. And yet what the man deposited is due to him in a sense, is it not?

— Yes.

— But it ought not to be returned when he demands it not being in his right mind.

— True, said he.

— It is then something other than this that Simonides must, as it seems, mean by the saying that it is just to render back what is due.

— Something else in very deed, he replied, for he believes that friends owe it to friends to do them some good and no evil.

— I see, said I; you mean that he does not render what is due or owing who returns a deposit of gold if this return and the acceptance prove harmful and the returner and the recipient are friends. Isn't that what you say Simonides means?

— Quite so.

— But how about this — should one not render to enemies what is their due?

— By all means, he said, what is due and owing to them, and there is due and owing from an enemy to an enemy what also is proper for him, some evil.

— It was a riddling definition of justice, then, that Simonides gave after the manner of poets; for while his meaning it seems, was that justice is rendering to each what befits him, the name that he gave to this was the due.

— What else do you suppose? said he.

— In heaven's name, said I, suppose someone had questioned him thus: Tell me, Simonides, the art that renders what is due and befitting to what is called the art of medicine? What do you take it would have been his answer?

— Obviously, he said, the art that renders to bodies drugs, foods, and drinks.

— And if he was asked the same question about cookery?

— It gives seasoning to meats.

— Good. In the same way, tell me the art that renders what to whom would be denominated justice?

— If we are to follow the previous examples, Socrates, it is that which renders benefits and harms to friends and enemies.

— To do good to friends and evil to enemies, then, is justice in his meaning?

— I think so.

— Who then is the most able when they are ill to benefit friends and harm enemies in respect to disease and health?

— The physician.

— And who navigates in respect of the perils of the sea?

— The pilot.

— Well then, the just man, in what action and for what work is he the most competent to benefit friends and harm enemies?

— In making war and as an ally, I should say.

— Very well. But now if they are not sick, friend Polemarchus, the physician is useless to them.

— True.

— And so to those who are not at sea the pilot.

— Yes.

— Shall we also say this that for those who are not at war the just man is useless?

— By no means.

— There is a use then even in peace for justice?

— Yes, it is useful.

— Then tell me, for the service and getting of what would you say that justice is useful in time of peace?

— In engagements and dealings, Socrates.

— And by dealings do you mean associations, partnerships, or something else?

— Associations, of course.

— Is it the just man then, who is a good and useful associate and partner in the placing of draughts or the draught-player?

— The player.

— And in the placing of bricks and stones is the just man a more useful and better associate than the builder?

— By no means.

— Then what is the association in which the just man is a better partner than the harpist as a harpist is better than the just man for striking the chords?

— For money-dealings, I think.

— Except, I presume, Polemarchus, for the use of money when there is occasion to buy in common or sell a horse. Then, I take it, the man who knows horses, isn't it so?

— Apparently.

— And again, if it is a vessel, the shipwright or the pilot.

— It would seem so. What then is the use of money in common for which a just man is the better partner?

— When it is to be deposited and kept safe, Socrates.

— You mean when it is to be put to no use but is to lie idle?

— Quite so.

— Then it is when money is useless that justice is useful in relation to it?

— It looks that way.

— And so you will have to say that when a shield and a lyre are to be kept and put to no use, justice is useful, but when they are to be made use of, the military art and music.

— Necessarily.

— And so in all other cases, in the use of each thing, justice is useless but in its uselessness useful?

— It looks that way. (Plato, *Republic*, 332a–333d.)

*The provisional conclusion of this argument is paradoxical. The crucial assumption seems to assimilate justice to typical technical craft-knowledge. But it is not made clear whether justice is on par with such distinct kinds of know-how, or crucially, different from them. The conclusion shows that under some interpretation 'giving each his due' leads to a paradox. This does not rule out other interpretations. Later, in the same dialogue, justice is shown to be giving each person what he is naturally fitted for, and thus, in another sense, his due. The idea that justice is a kind of theoretical (and practical) skill, is an application of the Socratic thesis that virtue, in its varied senses, is some kind of knowledge. If it is a specialized kind of knowledge, like ordinary skills, then we may wonder who, if anyone, has it, how it is to be acquired, and what use it will be.*

# 7

## THE HUMAN GOOD

### *The Virtues. Desiring the Good. Virtue is Knowledge.*

*Like many of his contemporaries, Socrates, turned from a study of natural science, to an investigation of man and his place in the world. Likened to a new Humanism, this interest coincided with the establishment of a democratic polity. Athens attracted thinkers from all over the Greek world and became the cultural hub of Greek civilization and manners. While Plato is careful to distinguish Socrates from his contemporaries, they share some common features, being interested in social and political issues. These intellectuals were generally dubbed 'sophists' — derived from the word sophos (wise man). Their interests ranged over a broad field, especially over ethics and politics. both of which were*

*contested fields. Aristotle confirms the move away from natural sciences to ethics and politics without directly implicating Socrates, while Xenophon distinguishes him from earlier thinkers.*

In Socrates's time an advance was made so far as the method was concerned; but at that time philosophers gave up the study of Nature and turned to the practical subject of 'goodness' and to political science. (Aristotle, *Parts of Animals*, 642a.)

Of those who worry about 'Universal Nature', some hold that 'what-is' is one (*Milesians*), others that it is infinite in number (*the Atomists*); some that all things are in perpetual motion (*Heraclitus*), others that nothing can ever be moved at any time (*Parmenides*); some that all life is birth and decay, others that nothing can ever be born or ever die (*Empedocles*). Nor were those the only questions he asked about such theorists. Students of human nature, he said, think that they will apply their knowledge in due course for the good of themselves and any others they choose. Do those who pry into heavenly phenomena imagine that, once they have discovered the laws by which these are produced, they will create at their will winds, waters, seasons, and such things to their need? Or have they no such expectation and are they satisfied with knowing the causes of these various phenomena? Such, then, was his criticism of those who meddle with these matters. His own conversation was ever of human things. The problems he discussed were, What is godly? What is ungodly? What is beautiful? What is ugly? What is just? What is unjust?

(Xenophon, *Memorabilia*, 1.1.16.)

*In Plato's Phaedo, as depicted by Aristophanes in* The Clouds, *Socrates admits that he did once, 'study nature' and physical causation but became disenchanted with mechanical explanations.*

*Socrates*: When I was young, Cebes, I was tremendously eager for the kind of wisdom which they call investigation of nature. I thought it was a glorious thing to know the causes of everything, why each thing comes into being and why it perishes and why it exists; and I was always unsettling myself with such questions as these: Do heat and cold, by a sort of fermentation, bring about the organization of animals, as some people say? Is it the blood, or air, or fire by which we think? Or is it none of these, and does the brain furnish the sensations of hearing and sight and smell, and do memory and opinion arise from these, and does knowledge come from memory and opinion in a state of rest? And again I tried to find out how these things perish, and I investigated the phenomena of heaven and earth until finally I made up my mind that I was by nature totally unfitted for this kind of investigation (Plato, *Phaedo*, 96b–c.)

## The Virtues

*The English term 'virtue' is frequently used to translate the Greek 'aretê' which has an equally dispersed range of meanings. 'Aretê' can also be translated as 'excellence', denoting any socially valued trait. The excellence of a horse or a warrior will be different. Many Sophists offered to teach virtue. Some described fighting in armour as a virtue/skill that could be taught. Others wondered whether aretê could be taught as skills are taught. The virtues that Socrates thought worth cultivating were what we would call moral virtues. Chief among them piety, self control, or moderation (sophrosune), courage, justice, and wisdom/knowledge. These last four are dubbed 'the cardinal virtues' in Plato's moral theory.*

### Moderation or Self-Control

*Moderation translates sophrosune, a character trait that includes a sense of modesty, forbearance, control of appetites, and, in women, chastity. Xenophon writes of Socrates:*

No less wonderful is it to me that some believed the charge brought against Socrates of corrupting the youth. In the first place, apart from what I have said, in control of his own passions and appetites he was the strictest of men; further, in endurance of cold and heat and every kind of toil he was most resolute and besides, his needs were so schooled to moderation that having very little he was yet very content. Such was his own character: How then can he have led others into impiety, crime, gluttony, lust, or sloth? On the contrary, he cured these vices in many, by putting into them a desire for goodness, and by giving them confidence that self-discipline would make them gentlemen. To be sure he never professed to teach this; but, by letting his own light shine, he led his disciples to hope that they through imitation of him would attain to such excellence. Furthermore, he himself never neglected the body, and reproved such neglect in others. Thus, overeating followed by overexertion he disapproved of. But he approved of taking as much hard exercise as is agreeable, for the habit not only insured good health, but did not hamper the care of the soul. On the other hand, he disliked foppery and pretentiousness in the fashion of clothes or shoes or in behaviour. (Xenophon, *Memorabilia*, 1.2.1–5.)

I recall in particular the substance of a conversation that he once had with Euthydemus on self-control.

— Tell me, Euthydemus, he said, do you think that freedom is a noble and splendid possession both for individuals and for communities?

— Yes, I think it is, in the highest degree.

— Then do you think that the man is free who is ruled by bodily pleasures and is unable to do what is best because of them?

— By no means.

— Possibly, in fact, to do what is best appears to you to be freedom, and so you think that to have masters who will prevent such activity is bondage?'And is it not likely that self-control causes actions the opposite of those that are due to lack of self-control?

— Certainly.

— Then is not the cause of the opposite actions presumably a very great blessing?

— Yes, presumably.

— Consequently we may presume, Euthydemus, that self-control is a very great blessing to a man?

— We may presume so, Socrates. (Xenophon, *Memorabilia*, 4.5.1–12.)

*In Plato's Gorgias, Callicles — a politician who despised the masses — admires the unbridled use of power and the pursuit of every pleasure. Socrates compares the life of the intemperate man with one who controls his impulses.*

*Callicles*: What do you mean by one who rules himself?

*Socrates*: Nothing recondite; merely what most people mean—one who is temperate and self-mastering, ruler of the pleasures and desires that are in himself.

Cal: ...I tell you now quite frankly... that he who would live rightly should let his desires be as strong as possible and not chasten them, and should be able to minister to them when they are at their height by reason of his manliness and intelligence, and satisfy each appetite in turn with what it desires.

*Soc*: Come now... consider if each of the two lives, the temperate and the licentious, might be described by imagining that each of two men had a number of jars, and those of one man were sound and full, one of wine, another of honey, a third of milk, and various others of various things, and that the sources of each of these supplies were scanty and difficult and only available through much hard toil: Well, one man, when he has taken his fill, neither draws off anymore nor troubles himself a jot, but remains at ease on that score; whilst the other finds, like his fellow, that the sources are possible indeed, though difficult, but his vessels are leaky and decayed, and he is compelled to fill them constantly, all night and day, or else suffer extreme distress. If such is the nature of each of the two lives, do you say that the licentious man has a happier one than the orderly? Do I, with this story of mine, induce you at all to concede that the orderly life is better than the licentious, or do I fail? (Plato, *Gorgias*, 493d–494a.)

***Courage***

*In Plato's dialogue named after the general Laches, Socrates discusses the nature of courage. While various definitions are rejected, the initial conversation shows the generality of Socrates's understanding of this virtue.*

*Socrates*: Then our first requisite is to know what virtue is? For surely, if we had no idea at all what virtue actually is, we could not possibly consult with anyone as to how he might best acquire it?

*Laches*: I certainly think not, Socrates.

*Soc*: Let us not, therefore, my good friend, inquire forthwith about the whole of virtue, since that may well be too much for us; but let us first see if we are sufficiently provided with knowledge about some part of it. In all likelihood this will make our inquiry easier.

*Lach*: Yes, let us do as you propose, Socrates.

*Soc*: Then which of the parts of virtue shall we choose? Clearly, I think, that which the art of fighting in armour is supposed to promote; and that, of course, is generally supposed to be courage, is it not?

*Lach*: Yes, it generally is, to be sure.

*Soc*: Then let our first endeavour be, Laches, to say what courage is: After that we can proceed to inquire in what way our young men may obtain it, in so far as it is to be obtained by means of pursuits and studies. Come, try and tell me, as I suggest, what is courage?

*Lach*: Socrates, that is nothing difficult: Anyone who is willing to stay at his post and face the enemy, and does not run away, you may be sure, is courageous.

...

*Soc*: Let us take that man to be courageous who, as you describe him yourself, stays at his post and fights the enemy.

*Lach*: I, for one, agree to that.

*Soc*: Yes, and I do too. But what of this other kind of man, who fights the enemy while fleeing, and not staying?

*Lach*: How fleeing?

*Soc*: Well, as the Scythians are said to fight, as much fleeing as pursuing.

*Lach*: (That's) the mode of the Scythian horsemen. That is the way of cavalry fighting; but with men-at-arms it is as I state it.

*Soc*: Except, perhaps, Laches, in the case of the Spartans. For they say that at Plataea, (*August 479 BCE where the combined Greek forces defeated the Persians*) when the Spartans came up to the men with wicker shields, they were not willing to stand and fight against these, but fled; when, however, the Persian ranks were broken, the Spartans kept turning round and fighting like cavalry, and so won that great battle.

*Lach*: What you say is true.

*Soc*: ...I wanted to have your view not only of brave men-at-arms, but also of courage in cavalry and in the entire warrior class; and of the courageous not only in war but in the perils of the sea, and all who in disease and poverty, or again in public affairs, are courageous; and further, all who are not merely courageous against pain or fear, but doughty fighters against desires and pleasures, whether standing their ground or turning back upon the foe — for I take it. Laches, there are courageous people in all these kinds.

*Lach*: Very much so, Socrates.

*Soc*: Then all these are courageous, only some have acquired courage in pleasures, some in pains, some in desires, and some in fears, while others, I conceive, have acquired cowardice in these same things.

*Lach*: To be sure. (Plato, *Laches*, 198a–199e.)

## *Justice*

*Justice was probably the most discussed political and ethical concept in the Greek tradition. Aristotle described it as the whole of virtue. Xenophon writes of a conversation Socrates had with the polymath, Hippias where he discusses written and unwritten laws:*

*Hippias*: As for justice, I feel confident that I can now say that which neither you nor anyone else can contradict.

*Socrates*: Upon my word, you mean to say that you have made a great discovery, if jurymen are to cease from voting different ways, citizens from disputing and litigation, and wrangling about the justice of their claims, cities from quarrelling about their rights and making war; and for my part, I don't see how to tear myself away from you till I have heard about your great discovery.

— But I vow you shall not hear unless you first declare your own opinion about the nature of justice; for it's enough that you mock at others, questioning and examining everybody, and never willing to render an account yourself or to state an opinion about anything.

— Indeed, Hippias! Haven't you noticed that I never cease to declare my notions of what is just?

— And how can you call that an account?

— I declare them by my deeds, anyhow, if not by my words. Don't you think that deeds are better evidence than words?

— Yes, much better, of course; for many say what is just and do what is unjust; but no one who does what is just can be unjust.

— Then have you ever found me dealing in perjury or calumny, or stirring up strife between friends or fellow-citizens, or doing any other unjust act?

— I have not.

— To abstain from what is unjust is just, don't you think?

— Even now, Socrates, you are clearly endeavouring to avoid stating what you think justice to be. You are saying not what the just do, but what they don't do.

— Well, I thought that unwillingness to do injustice was sufficient proof of justice.

But, if you don't think so, see whether you like this better: I say that what is lawful is just.

…

Laws, said Hippias, can hardly be thought of much account, Socrates, or observance of them, seeing that the very men who passed them often reject and amend them.

— Yes, said Socrates, and after going to war, cities often make peace again.

— To be sure.

— Then is there any difference, do you think, between belittling those who obey the laws on the ground that the laws may be annulled, and blaming those who behave well in the wars on the ground that peace may be made? Or do you really censure those who are eager to help their fatherland in the wars?

— No, of course not.

…

— Do you know what is meant by 'unwritten laws', Hippias?

— Yes, those that are uniformly observed in every country.

— Could you say that men made them?

— Nay, how could that be, seeing that they cannot all meet together and do not speak the same language?

— Then by whom have these laws been made, do you suppose?

— I think that the gods made these laws for men. For among all men the first law is to fear the gods.

— Is not the duty of honouring parents another universal law?

— Yes, that is another.

— And that parents shall not have sexual intercourse with their children nor children with their parents?

— No, I don't think that is a law of God.

— Why so?

— Because I notice that some transgress it.

— Yes, and they do many other things contrary to the laws. But surely the transgressors of the laws ordained by the gods pay a penalty that a man can in no wise escape, as some, when they transgress the laws ordained by man, escape punishment, either by concealment or by violence. (*Memorabilia*, 4.4.1–5 and 7–25.)

### *A Call to Virtue*

*Virtue said Socrates is the best condition of the soul. In Plato's* Apology, *Socrates makes clear the relation between virtue and care of the self.*

For I go about doing nothing else than urging you, young and old, not to care for your persons or your property more than for the perfection of your souls, or even so much; and I tell you that virtue does not come from money, but from virtue comes money and all other good things to man, both to the individual and to the state. (Plato, *Apology*, 30b.)

## Desiring the Good

*With an aim to identify the nature of virtue and what he means by it, Socrates begins with the observation that all men desire the good. While the claim might seem paradoxical, his argument is simple: by 'the good' Socrates simply means 'what is good for the person'. We might rephrase it by saying all men desire to do (or have done to them) what is beneficial or useful for them. Each man pursues his own good/interest. Differences arise because we see that there are different conceptions of what each person thinks is good for him. To resolve this Socrates tries to identify what it is that is really beneficial for a person as opposed to what people often mistake as their good. Socrates bases his ethical theory on what is later called rational self-interest. We should aim at what is really in our interest. The commonly regarded goods are neither good nor bad in themselves, but may be either misused or be the cause of misfortune: Is there anything that is an undisputed good? In conversation with Euthydemus as reported by Xenophon, Socrates questions the usual suspects:*

Well, said Socrates, I may assume, I take it, that you know what things are good and what are evil?

*Euthydemus*: Of course, for if I don't know so much as that, I must be worse than a slave.

— Come then, state them for my benefit.

— Well, that's a simple matter. First health in itself is, I suppose, a good, sickness an evil. Next the various causes of these two conditions meat, drink, habits are good or evil according as they promote health or sickness.

— Then health and sickness too must be good when their effect is good, and evil when it is evil.

— But when can health possibly be the cause of evil, or sickness of good?

— Why, in many cases; for instance, a disastrous campaign or a fatal voyage:the able-bodied who go are lost, the weaklings who stay behind are saved.

— True; but you see, in the successful adventures too the able-bodied take part, the weaklings are left behind.

— Then since these bodily conditions sometimes lead to profit, and sometimes to loss, are they any more good than evil?

— No, certainly not; at least so it appears from the argument. But wisdom now, Socrates, that at any rate is indisputably a good thing; for what is there that a wise man would not do better than a fool?

*Socrates*: Indeed! have you not heard how Daedalus was seized by Minos because of his wisdom, and was forced to be his slave, and was robbed of his country and his liberty, and essaying to escape with his son, lost the boy and could not save himself, but was carried off to the barbarians and again lived as a slave there?

...

— And how many others, do you suppose, have been kidnapped on account of their wisdom, and haled off to the great King's court, and live in slavery there?

— Happiness seems to be unquestionably a good, Socrates.

— It would be so, Euthydemus, were it not made up of goods that are questionable.

— But what element in happiness can be called in question?

— None, provided we don't include in it beauty or strength or wealth or glory or anything of the sort.

— But of course we shall do that. For how can anyone be happy without them?

— Then of course we shall include the sources of much trouble to mankind. For many are ruined by admirers whose heads are turned at the sight of a pretty face; many are led by their strength to attempt tasks too heavy for them, and meet with serious evils: many by their wealth are corrupted. (Xenophon, *Memorablia*, 4.2.30.)

*While the passage may suggest that Socrates is rejecting his preferred candidate, wisdom, as not always beneficial: The sort of wisdom or knowledge he cites in the case of Daedelus (the legendary master craftsman), is technical rather than moral knowledge. Accordingly, in his discussion with Meno, in Plato's dialogue of that name, he can take as a truism the fact that no one desires to suffer bad things.*

*Meno*: ...That, I say, is virtue — to desire what is honourable and be able to procure it.

*Soc*: Do you say that he who desires the honourable is desirous of the good?

*Meno*: Certainly.

*Soc*: Implying that there are some who desire what is bad, and others the good? Do not all men, in your opinion, my dear sir, desire the good?

*Meno*: I think not.

*Soc*: There are some who desire what is bad?

*Meno*: Yes.

*Soc*: Thinking what is bad to be good, do you mean, or actually recognizing it to be bad, and desiring it nevertheless?

*Meno*: Both, I believe.

*Soc*: Do you really believe, Meno, that a man knows what is bad to be bad, and still desires it?

*Meno*: Certainly.

*Soc*: What do you mean by 'desires'? Desires the possession of it?

*Meno*: Yes; what else could it be?

*Soc*: And does he think what is bad benefits him who gets it, or does he know that it harms him who has it?

*Meno*: There are some who think what is bad is a benefit, and others who know that it does harm.

*Soc*: And, in your opinion, do those who think what is bad a benefit, know that it is evil?

*Meno*: I do not think that at all.

*Soc*: Obviously those who are ignorant of what is bad do not desire it, but only what they supposed to be good, though it is really evil; so that those who are ignorant of it and think it good are really desiring the good. Is not that so?

*Meno*: It would seem to be so in their case.

*Soc*: Well now, I presume those who, as you say, desire what is bad, and consider that what is bad harms him who gets it, know that they will be harmed by it?

*Meno*: They needs must.

*Soc*: But do they not hold that those who are harmed are miserable in proportion to the harm they suffer? Then is there anyone who wishes to be miserable?

*Meno*: I do not suppose there is, Socrates.

*Soc*: No one, then, Meno, desires what is bad, if no one desires to be such an one: For what is being miserable but desiring what is bad and obtaining it?

*Meno*: It seems that what you say is true, Socrates, and that nobody desires what is bad. (Plato, *Meno*, 77b–78b.)

### Virtue and Other Goods

*For Socrates virtue is independent of external goods. If virtue is both necessary and sufficient for happiness as he thinks, then it would follow that all other so called goods were only conditionally and not absolutely, good. Here again, 'good' must be understood as 'good for the agent'. In Plato's dialogue, Socrates discusses this with Cleinias (a young and beautiful youth from the family of Alcibiades).*

*Socrates*: Do all we human beings wish to prosper? Or is this question one of the absurdities I was afraid of just now? For I suppose it is stupid merely to ask such things, since every man must wish to prosper.

— Everyone in the world, said Cleinias.

— Well then, I asked, as to the next step, since we wish to prosper, how can we prosper? Will it be if we have many good things? Or is this an even sillier question than the other? For surely this too must obviously be so.

He agreed.

— Come now, of things that are, what sort do we hold to be really good? Or does it appear to be no difficult matter, and no problem for an important person, to find here, too, a ready answer? Anyone will tell us that to be rich is good, surely?

— Quite true, he said.

— Then it is the same with being healthy and handsome, and having the other bodily endowments in plenty?

He agreed.

— Again, it is surely clear that good birth and talents and distinctions in one's own country are good things.

He admitted it.

— Then what have we still remaining, I asked, in the class of goods? What of being temperate, and just, and brave? I pray you tell me, Cleinias, do you think we shall be right in ranking these as goods, or in rejecting them? For it may be that someone will dispute it. How does it strike you?

— They are goods, said Cleinias.

— Very well, and where in the troupe shall we station wisdom? Among the goods?

— Among the goods.

— Then take heed that we do not pass over any of the goods that may deserve mention.

— I do not think we are leaving any out, said Cleinias.

— Hereupon I recollected one and said: Yes, by Heaven, we are on the verge of omitting the greatest of the goods.

— What is that? he asked.

— Good fortune, Cleinias: A thing which all men, even the worst fools, refer to as the greatest of goods. You are right, he said.

— Why, after putting good fortune in our former list, we have just been discussing the same thing again.

— What is the point?

— Surely it is ridiculous, when a thing has been before us all the time, to set it forth again and go over the same ground twice.

— To what are you referring? he asked.

— Wisdom, I replied, is presumably good fortune: even a child could see that.

Then I, perceiving his surprise, went on:

— Supposing you were, sick, with which kind of doctor would you like to venture yourself a wise one, or an ignorant?

— With a wise one.

— And your reason, I said, is this, that you would fare with better fortune in the hands of a wise one than of an ignorant one?

He assented.

— So that wisdom everywhere causes men to be fortunate: since I presume she could never err, but must needs be right in act and result; otherwise she could be no longer wisdom.

We came to an agreement somehow or other in the end that the truth in general was this: When wisdom is present, he with whom it is present has no need of good fortune as well. (Plato, *Euthydemus*, 278e–280b.)

***Knowledge and Happiness***

*Knowledge and virtue: While everyday instances of skills/knowledge are necessary (to achieve the ends of each of those skills), such knowledge falls short of the kind of knowledge that Socrates is interested in. In Plato's Charmides, Socrates supposes it to be moral knowledge (of good and evil). Here the meaning of the word good has changed, from what is beneficial to a person, it has become to what is good in itself: He will have to argue that they are identical.*

*Socrates*: by acting according to knowledge we should do well and be happy — this is a point which as yet we are unable to make out, my dear Critias.

— But still, he replied, you will have some difficulty in finding any other fulfilment of welfare if you reject the rule of knowledge.

— Then inform me further, on one more little matter. Of what is this knowledge? Do you mean of shoe-making?

— Good heavens, not I!

— Well, in wool, or in wood, or in something else of that sort ?

— No, indeed.

— Then we no longer hold, I said, to the statement that he who lives according to knowledge is happy;

for these workers, though they live according to knowledge, are not acknowledged by you to be happy: you rather admit the happy man, it seems to me, as one who lives according to knowledge about certain things; the sort of person who might know, besides what is to be, both every thing that has been and now is, and might be ignorant of nothing? Let us suppose such a man exists: you are not going to tell me, I am sure, of anyone alive who is yet more knowing than he.

— No, indeed.

— Then there is still one more thing I would fain know: Which of the sciences is it that makes him happy? Or does he owe it to all of them alike?

— By no means to all alike, he replied.

— But to which sort most? One that gives him knowledge of what thing, present, past or future? Is it that by which he knows draught-playing?

— Draught-playing indeed, he replied.

— Well, reckoning?

— By no means.

— Well, health?

— More likely, he said.

— And that science to which I refer as the most likely, gives him knowledge of what?

— Of good, he replied, and of evil. (Plato, *Charmides*, 174a–d.)

## Virtue is Knowledge

*This central Socratic thesis has been the subject of much discussion, its precise meaning has been hotly debated. Socrates seemed to identify all the virtues with knowledge, making knowledge itself the condition for them. Justice, courage, self-control, piety are dependent upon knowledge, as is, in consequence, happiness. Thrasymachus, in the* Republic, *complains about Socrates's identification of virtue with other positive traits.*

*Thrasymachus*: And don't you be telling me that it is that which ought to be, or the beneficial or the profitable or the gainful or the advantageous, but express clearly and precisely whatever you say. For I won't take from you any such drivel as that! (Plato, *Republic*, 336d.)

He said that justice and every other form of virtue is wisdom (*Sophia*). For just actions and all forms of virtuous activity are beautiful and good. He who knows the beautiful and good will never choose anything else, he who is ignorant of them cannot do them, and even if he tries, will fail. Hence the wise do what is beautiful and good, the unwise cannot and fail if they try. Therefore since just actions and all other forms of beautiful and good activity are virtuous actions, it is clear that justice and every other form of virtue is wisdom. (Xenophon, *Memorablia*, 3.9.5.)

*By connecting virtue with knowledge and so, seeing it like other technical skills, Socrates claims that it must be, at least in principle, teachable. In saying this Socrates is making both a democratic as well as aristocratic point: if virtue is teachable, then it is not innate nobility.*

*If it is teachable and involves expertise, then not everyone can have it equally. It's political relationship to the other skills, as the passage above implied, is that it must rule over them: without a moral rudder, technical know-how cannot lead to human flourishing (eudaimonia). In Plato's Meno, Socrates broadly connects virtue with knowledge.*

*Soc*: Well now, surely we call virtue a good thing, do we not, and our hypothesis stands, that it is good?

*Meno*: Certainly we do.

*Soc*: Then if there is some good, apart and separable from knowledge, it may be that virtue is not a kind of knowledge; but if there is nothing good that is not embraced by knowledge, our suspicion that virtue is a kind of knowledge would be well-founded.

*Meno*: Quite so.

*Soc*: Now it is by virtue that we are good?

*Meno*: Yes.

*Soc*: And if good, profitable; for all good things are profitable, are they not?

*Meno*: Yes.

*Soc*: So virtue is profitable?

*Meno*: That must follow from what has been admitted.

*Soc*: Then let us see, in particular instances, what sort of things they are that profit us.

Health, let us say, and strength, and beauty, and wealth these and their like we call profitable, do we not?

*Meno*: Yes.

*Soc*: But these same things, we admit, actually harm us at times; or do you dispute that statement?

*Meno*: No, I agree.

*Soc*: Consider now, what is the guiding condition in each case that makes them at one time profitable, and at another harmful. Are they not profitable *when the use of them is right*, and harmful when it is not?

*Meno*: To be sure.

*Soc*: Then let us consider next the *goods of the soul*: by these you understand temperance, justice, courage, intelligence, memory, magnanimity, and so forth?

*Meno*: Yes.

*Soc*: Now tell me; such of these as you think are not knowledge, but different from knowledge — do they not sometimes harm us, and sometimes profit us? For example, courage, if it is courage apart from prudence, and only a sort of boldness: When a man is bold without sense, he is harmed; but when he has sense at the same time, he is profited, is he not?

*Meno*: Yes.

*Soc*: And the same holds of temperance and intelligence: Things learnt and coordinated with the aid of sense are profitable, but without sense they are harmful?

*Meno*: Most certainly.

*Soc*: And in brief, all the undertakings and endurances of the soul, when guided by wisdom, end in happiness, but when folly guides, in the opposite.

*Meno*: That is so.

*Soc*: Then may we assert this *as a universal rule,* that in man all other things depend upon the soul, while the things of the soul herself depend upon wisdom, if they are to be good; and so by this account the profitable will be wisdom; and virtue, we say, is profitable?

*Meno*: Certainly,

*Soc*: Hence we conclude that *virtue is either wholly or partly wisdom*?

*Meno*: It seems to me that your statement, Socrates, is excellent.

*Soc*: Then if this is so, good men cannot be good by nature.

*Meno*: I think not.

*Soc*: No, for then, I presume, we should have had this result: If good men were so by nature, we surely should have had men able to discern who of the young were good by nature, and on their pointing them out we should have taken them over and kept them safe in the citadel, having set our mark on them far rather than on our gold treasure, in order that none might have tampered with them, and that when they came to be of age, they might be useful to their country.

*Meno*: Yes, most likely, Socrates.

*Soc*: So since it is not by nature that the good become good, is it by education?

*Meno*: We must now conclude, I think, that it is; and plainly, Socrates, on our hypothesis that virtue is knowledge, it must be taught. (Plato, *Meno*, 87e–88e.)

# 8

# THE SOCRATIC PARADOXES

## *No One Chooses Evil. Better to Be Harmed. Double Edge of Knowledge.*

*For Socrates, the claim that virtue is knowledge means that knowledge is the only thing worth cultivating. This does not refer to just any kind of knowledge, such as the technical craft-skills, but a distinct kind with its own proper subject matter. Such knowledge, its nature and subject largely underspecified in the early Platonic dialogues, is seen as representative of Socrates's own views. Clearly it is knowledge that discriminates between right and wrong. Knowledge of the good (and evil) was offered as a candidate in the discussion with Charmides, but such knowledge cannot immediately be identified with what is in the agent's own interest. Socrates confronts some paradoxical results that follow from this thesis. It*

*seems to do away with the usual candidates for morality, replacing feelings and emotions as the sources for our concern for ourselves and others with a calculating intellect. Further, the way such knowledge is understood seems to condemn everyone, including Socrates himself to a state of ignorance. For Socrates makes no distinction between degrees of knowledge. If you do not know you are ignorant. More charitably, it could be argued that being human means lacking the kind of super human knowledge Socrates holds up as his normative model. This would entail that the search for wisdom has no end and that no one can claim to know definitely what is right. Love of wisdom is the pursuit and not the possession of wisdom. That philosophers have been in search of a criterion for moral knowledge since then, perhaps proves that.*

*A summary account and critique of the Socratic thesis is given by Aristotle*

Accordingly Socrates thought that the aim is to get to know virtue, and he pursued an inquiry into the nature of justice and courage and each of the divisions of virtue. And this was a reasonable procedure, since he thought that all the virtues are forms of knowledge, so that knowing justice and being just must go together, for as soon as we have learnt geometry and architecture, we are architects and geometricians; owing to which he used to inquire what virtue is, but not how and from what sources it is produced. But although this does happen in the case of the theoretical sciences, inasmuch as astronomy and natural science and geometry have no other end except to get to know and to contemplate the nature of the things that are the subjects of the sciences (although it is true that they may quite possibly be useful to us accidentally for many of our necessary requirements), yet the aim of the productive sciences is something different from science and knowledge, for example the end of medicine is health and that of political science ordered government, or something of that sort, different from mere knowledge of the science. Although, therefore, it is fine even to attain a knowledge of the various fine things, all the same nevertheless in the case of goodness it is not the knowledge of its essential nature that is most valuable but the ascertainment of the sources that produce it. For our aim is not to know what courage is but to be courageous, not to know what justice is but to be just, in the same way as we want to be healthy rather than to ascertain what health is, and to be in good condition of body rather than to ascertain what good bodily condition is. (Aristotle, *Eudemian Ethics*, 1216b20.)

*Socrates might have responded, if you don't know what health is, how will you know if you are healthy? One who has such knowledge may well be a rarity. But given the possibility, we can understand the second paradox that Socrates is credited with: one who has this knowledge will never do wrong. All wrong doing is the result of ignorance. The Socratic paradox, no one does wrong willingly (knowingly) is noted by both Xenophon and Plato. In consequence, Socrates denies the possibility of weakness of the will (akrasia), often given as the reason why we fail so often to do what we know to be right. Several different reasons are given for such failure, passion, appetites and feelings of all kinds. But Socrates denies, in the face of facts, that knowledge can be dragged around like a slave.*

## No One Does Wrong Willingly

*Socrates provocatively denies the existence of akrasia, (roughly translated as 'weakness of will'). It is the condition when someone 'knows the better course and yet chooses the worse'. For Socrates this goes against the idea of rational self-interest. If knowledge is sufficient for virtue, and virtue necessary for happiness which is in sum the good of the agent and so the undisputed aim of all action, then no one, if he has knowledge (of the good) will, or more strongly can, act against his knowledge. In Xenophon, Socrates contrasts the self-controlled from the weak willed (acratic) in terms of pleasure. Self-control actually leads to greater physical pleasure. Here Socrates touches upon the law of diminishing returns applied to those who are overcome by desire:*

*Socrates*: Self-control is a very great blessing to a man?

— We may presume so, Socrates.

— Has it ever occurred to you, Euthydemus, that though pleasure is the one and only goal to which incontinence (*akrasia*) is thought to lead men, she herself cannot bring them to it, whereas nothing produces pleasure so surely as self control.

— How so?

— Incontinence will not let them endure hunger or thirst or desire or lack of sleep, which are the sole causes of pleasure in eating and drinking and sexual indulgence, and in resting and sleeping, after a time of waiting and resistance until the moment comes when these will give the greatest possible satisfaction; and thus she prevents them from experiencing any pleasure worthy to be mentioned in the most elementary and recurrent forms of enjoyment. But self-control alone causes them to endure the sufferings I have named, and therefore she alone causes them to experience any pleasure worth mentioning in such enjoyments.

Between wisdom and prudence he drew no distinction; but if a man knows and practises what is beautiful and good, knows and avoids what is base, that man he judged to be both wise and prudent. When asked further whether he thought that those who know what they ought to do and yet do the opposite are at once wise and vicious, he answered:

— No; not so much that, as both unwise and vicious. For I think that all men have a choice between various courses, and choose and follow the one which they think conduces most to their advantage. Therefore, I hold that those who follow the wrong course are neither wise nor prudent. (Xenophon, *Memorablia*, 3.9.4.)

*In Plato's Protagoras, Socrates argues more strongly, not only does the acratic or weak-willed have less pleasure than the self controlled, akrasia is actually impossible. That is, if one has the adequate knowledge which can measure the sum of pleasure and pain, no one would choose the greater pain over lesser pleasures. Socrates here is not advocating hedonism (the doctrine that pleasure is the only good), but showing that even on such an assumption, you still need to have recourse to knowledge in balancing short term with long term pleasure. Acrasia then is simply ignorance of what is in our best interest. This does not mean that people are not weak willed, but that they are weak willed because they are ignorant. The 'knowledge' that Socrates here invokes but does not discuss, is both calculating as well as action-guiding, something most people lack. Against the hedonists Socrates shows that their claim, that their better judgment is 'over come by pleasure', is absurd.* ***Here Socrates is offering a logical argument in defence of his paradox, ignoring the usual psychological explanations of 'weakness of the will.' For Socrates there is no gap between knowledge and practice.***

*Socrates*: Come, my good Protagoras, uncover some more of your thoughts: how are you in regard to knowledge? Do you share the view that most people take of this, or have you some other? The opinion generally held of knowledge is something of this sort: That it is no strong or guiding or governing thing; it is not regarded as anything of that kind, but people think that, while a man often has knowledge in him, he is not governed by it — but by something else — now by passion, now by pleasure, now by pain, at times by love, and often by fear; their feeling about knowledge is just what they have about a slave, that it may be dragged about by any other force. Now do you agree with this view of it, or do you consider that knowledge is something noble and able to govern man, and that whoever learns what is good and what is bad will never be swayed by anything to act otherwise than as knowledge bids, and that intelligence is a sufficient succour for mankind?

— Now you know that most people will not listen to you and me, but say that many, while *knowing what is best, refuse to perform it*, though they have the power, and do other things instead. And whenever I have asked them to tell me what can be the reason of this, they say that those who act so are acting under the influence of pleasure or pain, or under the control of one of the things I have just mentioned.

— Yes, Socrates, he replied, I regard this as but one of the many erroneous sayings of mankind.

*Socrates*: Come then, and join me in the endeavour to persuade the world and explain what is this experience of theirs, which they call being overcome by pleasure, and which they give as the reason why they fail to do what is best though they have knowledge of it. For perhaps if we said to them: What you assert, good people, is not correct, but *quite untrue* — they might ask us Protagoras and Socrates, if this experience is not being overcome by pleasure what on earth is it, and what do you call it? Tell us that the answer I should give them would be this: ...Do you not say that this thing occurs, good people, in the common case of a man being overpowered by the pleasantness of food or drink or sexual acts, and doing what he does though he knows it to be wicked? They would admit it.

Then you and I would ask them again: In what sense do you call such deeds wicked?

Is it that they produce those pleasures and are themselves pleasant at the moment, or that later on they cause diseases and poverty, and have many more such ills in store for us? Or, even though they have none of these things in store for a later day, and cause us only enjoyment, would they still be evil just because, forsooth, they cause enjoyment in some way or other? Can we suppose, Protagoras, that they will make any other answer than that these things are evil, not according to the operation of the actual pleasure of the moment, but owing to the later results in disease and those other ills?

— I think, said Protagoras, that most people would answer thus.

— Then in causing diseases they cause pains. They would admit this, I imagine. In causing poverty they cause pains?

— Then does it seem to you, my friends, that the only reason why these things are evil is that they end at last in pains, and deprive us of other pleasures? Would they admit this?

We both agreed that they would.

— Then again, suppose we should ask them the opposite: You, sirs, who tell us on the other hand that good things are painful — do you not give such instances as physical training, military service, and medical treatment conducted by cautery, incision, drugs, or starvation, and say that these are good, but painful? Would they not grant it?

He agreed that they would.

— Then do you call them good because they produce extreme pangs and anguish for the moment, or because later on they result in health and good bodily condition, the deliverance of cities, dominion over others, and wealth? They would assent to this, I suppose.

He agreed.

— And are these things good for any other reason than that they end at last in pleasures and relief and riddance of pains? Or have you some other end to mention, with respect to which you call them good, apart from pleasures and pains? They could not find one, I fancy.

— *Then do you pursue pleasure as being a good thing, and shun pain as being a bad one*?

He agreed that we do.

— So one thing you hold to be bad — pain; and pleasure you hold to be good, since the very act of enjoying you call bad as soon as it deprives us of greater pleasures than it has in itself, or leads to greater pains than the pleasures it contains. For if it is with reference to something else that you call the act of enjoyment bad, and with a view to some other end, you might be able to tell it us; but this you will be unable to do.

— I too think that they cannot, said Protagoras.

— Then is not the same thing repeated in regard

to the state of being pained? You call being pained a good thing as soon as it either rids us of greater pains than those it comprises, or leads to greater pleasures than its pains...

— Truly spoken, said Protagoras.

— Is it enough for you to live out your life pleasantly, without pain? If it is, and you are unable to tell us of any other good or evil that does not end in pleasure or pain, listen to what I have to say next. I tell you that if this is so, the argument becomes absurd, when you say that it is often the case that a man, knowing the evil to be evil, nevertheless commits it, when he might avoid it, because he is driven and dazed by his pleasures; while on the other hand you say that a man, knowing the good, refuses to do good because of the momentary pleasures by which he is overcome.

— The absurdity of all this will be manifest if we refrain from using a number of terms at once, such as pleasant, painful, good, and bad; and as there appeared *to be two things,* let us call them by two names—first, *good and evil*, and then later on, *pleasant and painful*. Let us then lay it down as our statement, that a man does evil in spite of knowing the evil of it.

— Now if someone asks us Why? We shall answer: Because he is overcome.

— By what? the questioner will ask us; and this time we shall be unable to reply: By pleasure — for this has exchanged its name for the good. So we must answer only with the words: Because he is overcome.

— By what? says the questioner.

— The good, must surely be our reply.

— Now if our questioner chance to be an arrogant person he will laugh and exclaim:

What a ridiculous statement, that a man does evil, knowing it to be evil, and not having to do it, because he is overcome by the good! Is this, he will ask, because the good is not worthy of conquering the evil in you, or because it is worthy?

— Clearly we must reply: Because it is not worthy otherwise he whom we speak of as overcome by pleasures would not have offended. But in what sense, he might ask us, is the good unworthy of the bad, or the bad of the good? This can only be when the one is greater and the other smaller, or when there are more on the one side and fewer on the other. We shall not find any other reason to give.

— So it is clear, he will say, that by 'being overcome' you mean getting the greater evil in exchange for the lesser good. That must be agreed. Then let us apply the terms pleasant and painful to these things instead, and say that a man does what we previously called evil, but now call painful, knowing it to be painful, because he is overcome by the pleasant, which is obviously unworthy to conquer.

— What unworthiness can there be in pleasure as against pain, save an excess or defect of one compared with the other? That is, when one becomes greater and the other smaller, or when there are more on one side and fewer on the other, or here a greater degree and there a less. For if you should say: But, Socrates, the immediately pleasant differs widely from the subsequently pleasant or painful, I should reply:

Do they differ in anything but pleasure and pain? That is the only distinction. Like a practised weigher, put pleasant things and painful in the scales, and with them the nearness and the remoteness, and tell me which count for more. For if you weigh pleasant things against pleasant, the greater and the more are always to be preferred: if painful against painful, then always the fewer and smaller. If you weigh pleasant against painful, and find that the painful are out-balanced by the pleasant — whether the near by the remote or the remote by the near — you must take that course of action to which the pleasant are attached; but not that course if the pleasant are outweighed by the painful. Can the case be otherwise, I should ask, than thus, my friends?

To this he too assented.

— Since that is the case, then, I shall say, please answer me this: Does not the same size appear larger to your sight when near, and smaller when distant? They will admit this. And it is the same with thickness and number? And sounds of equal strength are greater when near, and smaller when distant? They would agree to this.

— Now if our welfare consisted in doing and choosing things of large dimensions, and avoiding and not doing those of small, what would be our salvation in life?

Would it be the art of measurement, or the power of appearance? Is it not the latter that leads us astray, as we saw, and many a time causes us to take things topsy-turvy and to have to change our minds both in our conduct and in our choice of great or small? Whereas the art of measurement would have made this appearance ineffective, and by showing us the truth would have brought our soul into the repose of abiding by the truth, and so would have saved our life. Would men acknowledge, in view of all this, that the art which saves our life is measurement, or some other?

It is measurement, he agreed.

...

— Well then, my friends, since we have found that the salvation of our life depends on making a right choice of pleasure and pain — of the more and the fewer, the greater and the smaller, and the nearer and the remoter — is it not evident, in the first place, that measurement is a study of their excess and defect and equality in relation to each other?

And being measurement, I presume it must be an art or science?

Well, the nature of this art or science we shall consider some other time; but the mere fact of its being a science will suffice for the proof which Protagoras and I are required to give in answer to the question you have put to us.

You asked it, if you remember, when we were agreeing that there is nothing stronger than knowledge, and that knowledge, wherever it may be found, has always the upper hand of pleasure or anything else; and then you said that pleasure often masters even the man of knowledge, and on our refusing to agree with you, you went on to ask us:

Protagoras and Socrates, if this experience is not 'being overcome by pleasure' whatever can it be. and what do you call it? Tell us.

If on the spur of the moment we had replied, Ignorance, you would have laughed us to scorn: But now if you laugh at us you will be laughing at yourselves as well. For you have admitted that *it is from defect of knowledge that men err*, when they do err, in their choice of pleasures and pains — that is, in the choice of good and evil and from defect not merely of knowledge but of the knowledge which you have now admitted also to be that of measurement. And surely you know well enough for yourselves that the erring act committed without knowledge is done through ignorance. Accordingly 'to be overcome by pleasure' means just this — ignorance in the highest degree. (Plato, *Protagoras*, 352b–357d.)

*The direct challenge to Socrates's denial of akrasia was made by his contemporary. The playwright Euripides who has at least two characters affirm that despite knowing what they are doing is wrong, they are overcome (not by pleasure) by passion. In Euripides's tragedy, the* Phaedra, *overcome by desire for her chaste stepson, Phaedra cries out: 'We know and recognize what is right, but we do not act on it, for we are in the grip of passion' (Euripides,* Phaedra, *line. 380.) Medea, in the play named after her voices similar sentiments as she decides to kill her children to spite her husband. Future pains are difficult to measure against present pleasures because we do not experience them, even as we often ignore their probable outcome.*

## Better to Be Harmed than to Do Harm

*If one cannot willingly (knowingly) act against one's own interest, what about cases where one is doing wrong to others by harming them? Acting justly is understood as 'another's good'. Being just is often not in the agent's interest. How can Socrates argue that it is never in one's interest to act unjustly (harming others)? Yet this is what Socrates holds in Plato's Crito while in jail awaiting execution. It is never right to act unjustly. Such sentiments would certainly been an anathema to the outlook of the times (or of any times), as he notes.*

*Socrates*: Ought we in no way to do wrong (injustice) intentionally, or should we do wrong in some ways but not in others? Or, as we often agreed in former times, is it never right or honourable to do wrong? Is not wrongdoing inevitably an evil and a *disgrace to the wrongdoer*? Do we believe this or not?

*Crt*: We do.

*Soc*: Then we ought not to do wrong at all.

*Crt*: Why, no.

*Soc*: And we ought not even to requite wrong with wrong, as the world thinks, since we must not do wrong at all.

*Crt*: Apparently not.

*Soc*: Well, Crito, ought one to do evil or not?

*Crt*: Certainly not, Socrates.

*Soc*: Well, is it right to requite evil with evil, as the world says it is, or not right ?

*Crt*: Not right, certainly.

*Soc*: For doing evil to people is the same thing as wronging them.

*Crt*: That is true.

*Soc*: Then we ought neither to requite wrong with wrong nor to do evil to anyone, *no matter what he may have done to us*. And be careful, Crito, that you do not, in agreeing to this, agree to something you do not believe for *I know that there are few who believe or ever will believe this. Now those who believe this, and those who do not, have no common ground of discussion, but they must necessarily, in view of their opinions, despise one another*. Do you therefore consider very carefully whether you agree and share in this opinion, and let us take as the starting point of our discussion the assumption that it is never right to do wrong or to requite wrong with wrong, or when we suffer evil to defend ourselves by doing evil in return. Or do you disagree and refuse your assent to this starting point? For I have long held this belief and I hold it yet, but if you have reached any other conclusion, speak and explain it to me. (Plato, *Crito*, 49a.)

*Socrates, in Plato's* Gorgias, *extends this principle to claim that it is actually better (for the agent) to suffer injustice than to do it. Socrates himself of course is an example of someone who suffering an unjust penalty, chose not to act unjustly (escaping from prison). Socrates, as we may notice, using dual sets: 'honourable and disgraceful', 'good and evil', 'pleasant and painful', 'useful and pleasurable', puts Polus on the mat. However, he slides between what is painful for those who suffer injustice and those who are spectators of acts of injustice. The latter are not physically pained, though they may be distressed viewing injustice done to others: for them, doing injustice may still be disgraceful but it will not be more painful than seeing others suffer it.*

*Socrates*: Yes, indeed, Polus, that is my doctrine; the men and women who are gentle and good are also happy, as I maintain, and the unjust and evil are miserable... For I certainly think that I and you and every man do really believe, that *to do is a greater evil than to suffer injustice*: And not to be punished than to be punished.

...Tell me then, which of the two, Polus, in your opinion, is the worst? To do injustice or to suffer?

*Polus*: I should say that suffering was worst.

*Soc*: And which is the greater disgrace? Answer.

*Polus*: To do.

*Soc*: And the greater disgrace is the greater evil?

*Polus*: Certainly not.

*Soc*: I understand you to say, if I am not mistaken, that the honourable is not the same as the good, or the disgraceful as the evil?

*Polus*: Certainly not.

*Soc*: Let me ask a question of you: When you speak of beautiful things, such as bodies, colours, figures, sounds, institutions, do you not call them beautiful in reference to some standard: Bodies, for example, are beautiful (*kalos*) in proportion *as they are useful*, or as the sight of them *gives pleasure to the spectators*. Can you give any other account of personal beauty?

*Polus*: I cannot.

*Soc*: And you would say of figures or colours generally that they were beautiful, either by reason of the *pleasure* which they give, or of their *use*, or of both?

...Laws and institutions also have no beauty (*kalos*) in them except in so far as they are useful or pleasant or both?

*Polus*: I think not.

*Soc*: And may not the same be said of the beauty (nobility) of knowledge?

*Polus*: To be sure, Socrates; and I very much approve of your measuring beauty by the standard of *pleasure* and *utility*.

*Soc*: And deformity or disgrace may be equally measured by the opposite standard of *pain* and *evil*?

*Polus*: Certainly.

*Soc*: Then when of two beautiful things one exceeds in beauty, the measure of the excess is to be taken in one or both of these; that is to say, in pleasure or utility or both?

*Polus*: Very true.

*Soc*: And of two deformed things, that which exceeds in deformity or disgrace, exceeds either in pain or evil — must it not be so?

*Polus*: Yes.

*Soc*: But then again, what was the observation which you just now made, about doing and suffering wrong?

Did you not say, that suffering wrong was more evil, and doing wrong more disgraceful?

*Polus*: I did.

*Soc*: Then, if doing wrong is more disgraceful than suffering, the more disgraceful must be more painful and must exceed in pain or in evil or both does not that also follow?

*Polus*: Of course.

*Soc*: First, then, let us consider whether the doing of injustice exceeds the suffering in the consequent pain. Do the injurers suffer more than the injured?

*Polus*: No, Socrates; certainly not.

*Soc*: Then they do not exceed in pain?

*Polus*: No.

*Soc*: But if not in pain, then not in both?

*Polus*: Certainly not.

*Soc*: Then they can only exceed in the other?

*Polus*: Yes.

*Soc*: That is to say, in evil?

*Polus*: True.

*Soc*: Then doing injustice will have an excess of evil, and will therefore be a greater evil than suffering injustice?

*Polus*: Clearly.

*Soc*: But have not you and the world already agreed that to do injustice is more disgraceful than to suffer?

*Polus*: Yes.

*Soc*: And that is now discovered to be more evil?

*Polus*: True.

*Soc*: And would you prefer a greater evil or a greater dishonour to a less one?

*Polus*: I should say no.

*Soc*: Would any other man prefer a greater to a less evil?

*Polus*: No, not according to this way of putting the case, Socrates.

*Soc*: Then I said truly, Polus, that neither you, nor I, nor any man, would rather do than suffer injustice; for to do injustice is the greater evil of the two.

*Polus*: That is the conclusion. (Plato, *Gorgias*, 470e–475e.)

*But what, if any, are the advantages of acting justly? How can justice (not harming others) be in the agent's interest? In the first book of the* Republic, *reminiscent of Socratic argumentative methods, Thrasymachus articulates the standard view that one must help one's friends and harm one's enemies.*

*Thrasymachus*: And you are so far out concerning the just and justice and the unjust and injustice that you don't know that justice and the just are literally the other fellow's good — the advantage of the stronger and the ruler, but a detriment of the subject who obeys and serves; while injustice is the contrary and rules those who are simple in every sense of the word and just, and they being thus ruled do what is for his advantage who is the stronger and make him happy.

*Socrates*: I tell you for my part that I am not convinced, neither do I think that injustice is more profitable than justice, not even if one gives it free scope and does not hinder it of its will. But, suppose, sir, a man to be unjust and to be able to act unjustly either because he is not detected or can maintain it by violence, all the same he does not convince me that it is more profitable than justice. (Plato, *Republic*. 343c, 345a.)

*Socrates's response is in two parts: firstly rulers, like other craftsmen, rule in the interest of the ruled (and not in their self-interest). His argument here is hardly convincing, but can be supported by stipulating that rulers are those who rule as rulers ought to. Secondly, Socrates looks at the claim that injustice is more profitable for the individual than justice — as long as one can remain undetected. Crime, a modern Thrasymachus would argue, if undetected, pays. The argument resumes with the summary position restated: Justice (acting rightly) is identified with a form of moral consistency: Co-operation is necessary for any action that is to the advantage of both cities and individuals.*

*Socrates*: What is the nature of injustice as compared with justice? For the statement made, I believe, was that injustice is a more potent and stronger thing than justice. But now, I said, if justice is wisdom and virtue, it will easily, I take it, be shown to be also a stronger thing than injustice, since injustice is ignorance — no one could now fail to recognize that — but what I want is not quite so simple as that. I wish, Thrasymachus, to consider it in some such fashion as this. A city, you would say, may be unjust and try to enslave other cities unjustly, have them enslaved and hold many of them in subjection...The point that I am considering is this, whether the city that thus shows itself superior to another will have this power without justice or whether she must of necessity combine it with justice....And tell me this: Do you think that a city, an army, or bandits, or thieves, or any other group that attempted any action in common, could accomplish anything if they wronged one another? If *it is the business of injustice to engender hatred wherever it is found*, will it not, when it springs up either among freemen or slaves, cause them to hate and be at strife with one another, and make them incapable of effective action in common? In the individual too, I presume, its presence will operate all these effects which it is its nature to produce. It will in the first place make him incapable of accomplishing anything because of inner faction and lack of self-agreement, and then an enemy to himself and to the just. (Plato, *Republic*. 343c–351e.)

## The Paradox of Knowledge

*While doing wrong or acting unjustly is not an advantage, yet Socrates argues, paradoxically, that those who do wrong knowingly are better than those who act in ignorance. Socrates makes this outrageous claim in Plato's Lesser Hippias, which may not be an authentic work of Plato's, but is nevertheless consistent with what he writes elsewhere.*

*Socrates*: For I maintain that those who hurt or injure mankind, and speak falsely and deceive, and err voluntarily, are better far than those who do wrong involuntarily… In general those who do wrong involuntarily are worse than those who do wrong voluntarily… I am very desirous, Hippias, of examining this question, as to *which are the better — those who err voluntarily or involuntarily*? And if you will answer me, I think that I can put you in the way of approaching the subject: You would admit, would you not, that there are good runners?

*Hipp*: Yes.

*Soc*: And there are bad runners?

*Hipp*: Yes.

*Soc*: And he who runs well is a good runner, and he who runs ill is a bad runner?

*Hipp*: Very true.

*Soc*: And he who runs slowly runs ill, and he who runs quickly runs well?

*Hipp*: Yes.

*Soc*: Then in a race, and in running, swiftness is a good, and slowness is an bad quality?

*Hipp*: To be sure.

*Soc*: Which of the two then is a better runner? He who runs slowly voluntarily, or he who runs slowly involuntarily?

*Hipp*: He who runs slowly voluntarily.

*Soc*: And is not running a species of doing?

*Hipp*: Certainly.

*Soc*: And if a species of doing, a species of action?

*Hipp*: Yes.

*Soc*: Then he who runs badly does a bad and dishonourable action in a race?

*Hipp*: Yes; a bad action, certainly.

*Soc*: And he who runs slowly runs badly?

*Hipp*: Yes.

*Soc*: Then the good runner does this bad and disgraceful action voluntarily, and the bad involuntarily?

*Hipp*: That is to be inferred.

*Soc*: Then he who involuntarily does bad actions, is worse in a race than he who does them voluntarily?

*Hipp*: Yes, in a race.

*Soc*: And what would you say of the characters of slaves? Should we not prefer to have those who voluntarily do wrong and make mistakes, and are they not better in their mistakes than those who commit them involuntarily?

*Hipp*: Yes.

*Soc*: And should we not desire to have our own minds in the best state possible?

*Hipp*: Yes.

*Soc*: And will our minds be better if they do wrong and make mistakes voluntarily or involuntarily?

*Hipp*: O, Socrates, it would be a monstrous thing to say that those who do wrong voluntarily are better than those who do wrong involuntarily!

*Soc*: *But if justice be power as well as knowledge* — then will not the soul which has both knowledge and power be the more just, and that which is the more ignorant be the more unjust? Must it not be so?

*Hipp*: Clearly.

*Soc*: And is not the soul which has the greater power and wisdom also better, and better able to do both good and evil in every action?

*Hipp*: Certainly.

*Soc*: The soul, then, which acts ill, acts voluntarily by power and knowledge — and these, either one or both of them are elements of justice?

*Hipp*: That seems to be true.

*Soc*: And to do injustice is to do ill, and not to do injustice is to do well?

*Hipp*: Yes.

*Soc*: And will not the better and abler soul when it does wrong, do wrong voluntarily, and the bad soul involuntarily?

*Hipp*: Clearly.

*Soc*: And the good man is he who has the good soul, and the bad man is he who has the bad?

*Hipp*: Yes.

*Soc*: Then the good man will voluntarily do wrong, and the bad man involuntarily, if the good man is he who has the good soul?

*Hipp*: Which he certainly has.

*Soc*: Then, Hippias, he who voluntarily does wrong and disgraceful things, *if there be such a man*, will be the good man?

*Hipp*: There I cannot agree with you.

*Soc*: Nor can I agree with myself, Hippias; and yet that seems to be the conclusion which, as far as we can see at present, must follow from our argument. (*Hippias Minor*, 374–375.)

*Socrates is not saying that the man who knows what is right will do what is wrong.*

*His point is that only one who knows what is right will know what is not right and can do that, as a result of his knowledge. The man who does not know what is right and in his interest, when he acts against his own interest and does something wrong, will do so involuntarily. He acts out of ignorance of his own interest, as argued in the denial of acrasia. In the matter of technical skills, only the one who knows can consistently misuse his knowledge. If moral knowledge is like a skill, the just man will be best able to consistently and effectively act unjustly. At the end of the conversation, it remains open whether Socrates is committed or not to such a radical separation of knowledge and ignorance.*

# 9

# TRIAL AND EXECUTION

## *Against Democracy. Socrates's Defence. His Last Words.*

*In the spring of 399 BCE, Socrates was was accused of impiety: worshipping strange gods and corrupting the youth. There were no direct political charges against him because of an amnesty declared soon after the restoration of the democracy in 403 BCE. Meletus was the chief accuser, seconded by the more influential Anytus, a former general, who had been active in the overthrow of the oligarchs. A third accuser was one Lycon, a democrat, whose son had been executed during the Oligarchy. Many of the oligarchs who took control of the city had been associated with Socrates — Critias and Charmides were Plato's relatives; Alcibiades was regarded as both a traitor and guilty of sacrilege. Both*

*Critias and Charmides had been killed and Alcibiades had fled, first to Sparta, then to Persia (both enemies of Athens). The trial and subsequent execution of Socrates, has been seen as a way for the re-established democracy to publicly punish someone, despite the amnesty declared earlier.*

## Opposition to Democracy

*Although not an explicit charge against him, Socrates was thought to be opposed to the democracy. Xenophon obliquely tries to respond to that charge, while Plato, using the idea of expertise and technical craft-knowledge as a paradigm, connects Socrates's use of everyday workmen as examples of expertise to put a question mark against typical democratic procedures.*

*Socrates* (to Euthydemus): as the state you are preparing yourself to direct is governed by the people, no doubt you know what popular government (*demokratia*) is?

*Euthydemus*: I think so, certainly.

— Then do you suppose it possible to know popular government without knowing the people (*demos*)? Of what do you suppose it to consist?

— The poorer classes, I presume.

— You know the poor, then?

— Of course I do.

— And you know the rich too?

— Yes, just as well as the poor.

— What kind of men do you call poor and rich?

— The poor, I imagine, are those who have not enough to pay for what they want; the rich those who have more than enough.

— Have you observed, then, that some who have very little not only find it enough, but even manage to save out of it, whereas others cannot live within their means, however large?

— Yes, certainly thanks for reminding me I know, in fact, of some despots even who are driven to crime by poverty, just like paupers.

— Therefore, if that is so, we will include despots in the people, and men of small means, if they are thrifty, in the rich.

— I am forced to agree once more, cried Euthydemus, very dejected.

(Xenophon, *Memorablia*, 4.2.36–38.)

*The democratic assembly gave opportunity to citizens to speak in favour or against proposed legislation, before voting took place. Socrates like many others thought that this gave undue voice and weight to the ignorant opinions of the masses. The accuser here is thought to be Polycrates. Though this charge is not part of the official indictment, Socrates's opposition to democratic procedures, like random selection by lot, a way many officials were appointed, was well known. So too was his frequent use of expert craft-knowledge as a model for political wisdom.*

But, said his accuser, he taught his companions to despise the established laws by insisting on the folly of appointing public officials by lot, when none would choose a pilot or builder or flautist by lot, nor any other craftsman for work in which mistakes are far less disastrous than mistakes in statecraft. Such sayings, he argued, led the young to despise the established constitution and made them violent. (Ibid. 1.2.9–10.)

*Socrates*: I say, in common with the rest of the Greeks, that the Athenians are wise. Now I observe, when we are collected for the Assembly, and the city has to deal with an affair of building, we send for builders to advise us on what is proposed to be built; and when it is a case of laying down a ship, we send for shipwrights; and so in all other matters which are considered learnable and teachable. But if anyone else, whom the people do not regard as a craftsman, attempts to advise them, no matter how handsome and wealthy and well-born he may be, not one of these things induces them to accept him; they merely laugh him to scorn and shout him down, until either the speaker retires from his attempt, overborne by the clamour, or the stewerds pull him from his place or turn him out altogether by order of the chair. Such is their procedure in matters which they consider professional. But when they have to deliberate on something connected with the administration of the State, the man who rises to advise them on this may equally well be a smith, a shoemaker, a merchant, a sea-captain, a rich man, a poor man, of good family or of none, and nobody thinks of casting in his teeth, as one would in the former case, that his attempt to give advice is justified by no instruction obtained in any quarter, no guidance of any master. (Plato, *Protagoras*, 319b.)

*Cases like these came to the court of the King Archon — the chief magistrate, only nominally called a king. Socrates's case was decided by a jury of 501. All trials in Athens lasted a single day. First the prosecution read the charges, then the defendant responded; the jury voted for guilt or acquittal.There were no intermediaries, the accuser and accused had to speak on their own behalf. If the accuser did not receive a fifth of the votes, he was fined.*

*If the accused was found guilty, the prosecution proposed a penalty (in Socrates's case death); the defence a counter-penalty (a fine or exile were the most common). The jury voted again to choose between these. At this stage the jury could neither change its verdict nor refuse to choose between the proposed penalties. Xenophon's version is thought to contain a response to the prosecution's speech which emphasised Socrates's anti-democratic teaching, the subject of Polycrates's indictment.*

## Socrates's Defence

*It is not known when Xenophon's* Apology *(Defence) was written, but by then both Socrates and Anytus were dead, and other accounts of the trial had appeared. Hermogenes, the authority on whom Xenophon relied, had been in the Socratic circle. Although not mentioned in Plato's* Apology, *in the Phaedo he is said to have been with Socrates at the time of his execution, and so may be presumed to have first hand knowledge of the trial. Xenophon writes:*

It seems to me fitting to hand down to memory, furthermore, how Socrates, on being indicted, deliberated on his defence and on his end. It is true that others have written about this, and that all of them have reproduced the loftiness of his words, a fact which proves that his utterance really was of the character intimated; but they have not shown clearly that he had now come to the conclusion that for him death was more to be desired than life; and hence his lofty utterance appears rather ill considered. Hermogenes was a companion of his and has given us reports of such a nature as to show that the sublimity of his speech was appropriate to the resolve he had made. For he stated that on seeing Socrates discussing any and every subject rather than the trial, he had said:

*Hermogenes*: Socrates, ought you not to be giving some thought to what defence you are going to make?

*Socrates*: Why, do I not seem to you to have spent my whole life in preparing to defend myself?

Then when he asked: How so? he had said,

— Because all my life I have been guiltless of wrong-doing; and that I consider the finest preparation for a defence.

*Hermogenes*: Do you not observe that the Athenian courts have often been carried away by an eloquent speech and have condemned innocent men to death, and often on the other hand the guilty have been acquitted either because their plea aroused compassion or because their speech was witty?

*Soc*: Yes, indeed; I have tried twice already to meditate on my defence, but my divine sign interposes.

And when Hermogenes observed: That is a surprising statement, he had replied,

— Do you think it surprising that even God holds it better for me to die now? Do you not know that I would refuse to concede that any man has lived a better life than I have up to now? For I have realized that my whole life has been spent in righteousness toward God and man, a fact that affords the greatest satisfaction; and so I have felt a deep self-respect and have discovered that my associates hold corresponding sentiments toward me. But now, if my years are prolonged, I know that the frailties of old age will inevitably be realized, that my vision must be less perfect and my hearing less keen, that I shall be slower to learn and more forgetful of what I have learned. If I perceive my decay and take to complaining, how could I any longer take pleasure in life?

Perhaps, God in his kindness is taking my part and securing me the opportunity of ending my life not only in season but also in the way that is easiest. For if I am condemned now, it will clearly be my privilege to suffer a death that is adjudged by those who have superintended this matter to be not only the easiest but also the least irksome to one's friends and one that implants in them the deepest feeling of loss for the dead. For when a person leaves behind in the hearts of his companions no remembrance to cause a blush or a pang, but dissolution comes while he still possesses a sound body and a spirit capable of showing kindliness, how could such a one fail to be sorely missed?

Hermogenes stated that with this resolve Socrates came before the jury after his adversaries had *charged him with not believing in the gods worshipped by the state and with the introduction of new deities in their stead and with corruption of the young*, and replied:

— One thing that I marvel at in Meletus, gentlemen, is what may be the basis of his assertion that 1 do not believe in the gods worshipped by the state; for all who have happened to be near at the time, as well as Meletus himself, if he so desired, have seen me sacrificing at the communal festivals and on the public altars. As for introducing new divinities how could I be guilty of that merely in asserting that a voice of God is made manifest to me indicating my duty? Surely those who take their opinions from the cries of birds and the utterances of men form their judgments on 'voices'. Will any one dispute either that thunder utters its 'voice', or that it is an one of the greatest moment? Does not the very priestess who sits on the tripod at Delphi divulge the god's will through a 'voice'?

More than this of course was said both by Socrates himself and by the friends who joined in his defence. But I have not made it a point to report the whole trial; rather I am satisfied to make it clear that while Socrates's whole concern was to keep free from any act of impiety toward the gods or any appearance of wrong-doing toward man, he did not think it meet to beseech the jury to let him escape death; instead, he believed that the time had now come for him to die. This conviction of his became more evident than ever after the adverse issue of the trial. For, first of all, when he was bidden to name his penalty, he refused personally and forbade his friends to name one, but said that naming the penalty in itself implied an acknowledgement of guilt.

Then, when his companions wished to remove him clandestinely from prison, he would not accompany them, but seemed actually to banter them, asking them whether they knew of any spot outside of Attica that was inaccessible to death.

When the trial was over, Socrates (according to Hermogenes) remarked:

— Well, gentlemen, those who instructed the witnesses that they must bear false witness against me, perjuring themselves to do so, and those who were won over to do this must feel in their hearts a guilty consciousness of great impiety and iniquity; but as for me, why should my spirit be any less exalted now than before my condemnation, since I have not been proved guilty of having done any of the acts mentioned in the of indictment? ...And so it seems astonishing to me how you could ever have been convinced that I had committed an act meriting death. But further, my spirit need not be less exalted because I am to be executed unjustly; for the ignominy of that attaches not to me but to those who condemned me.

*— And I know that time to come as well as time past will attest that I, too, far from ever doing any man a wrong or rendering him more wicked, have rather profited those who conversed with me by teaching them, without reward, every good thing that lay in my power.*

With these words he departed, blithe in glance, in mien, in gait, as comported well indeed with the words he had just uttered. When he noticed that those who accompanied him were in tears, 'What is this?' Hermogenes reports him as asking.

— Are you just now beginning to weep? Have you not known all along that from the moment of my birth nature had condemned me to death?

A man named Apollodorus, who was there with him, a very ardent disciple of Socrates, but otherwise simple, exclaimed: But, Socrates, what I find it hardest to bear is that I see you being put to death unjustly! Stroking Apollodorus's head, he is said to have replied: My beloved Apollodorus, was it your preference to see me put to death justly? and smiled as he asked the question.

...And so, in contemplating the man's wisdom and nobility of character, I find it beyond my power to forget him or, in remembering him, to refrain from praising him.

And if among those who make virtue their aim any one has ever been brought into contact with a person more helpful than Socrates, I count that man worthy to be called most blessed. (Xenophon, *Apology*, selections)

*In Plato's* Apology, *we are only given the two speeches of Socrates, the first defending himself against the accusations, the second in response to the verdict, proposing an alternative to death. The first verdict had only a margin of 30 votes against him, the second, for death, an overwhelming majority. We have already given some of the passages from the first speech earlier. Here is the substance of the final speech where Socrates proposes an alternative penalty to death: free maintenance at state expense.*

*Socrates*: I am not grieved, men of Athens, at this vote of condemnation you have cast against me, and that for many reasons, among them the fact that your decision was not a surprise to me. I am much more surprised by the number of votes for and against it; for I did not expect so small a majority, but a large one. Now, it seems, if only thirty votes had been cast the other way, I should have been acquitted. And so, I think, so far as Meletus is concerned, I have even now been acquitted, and not merely acquitted, but anyone can see that, if Anytus and Lycon had not come forward to accuse me, he would have been fined a thousand drachmas for not receiving a fifth part of the votes. And so the man proposes the penalty of death.

Well, then, what shall I propose as an alternative? Clearly that which I deserve, shall I not? And what do I deserve to suffer or to pay, because in my life I did not keep quiet, but neglecting what most men care for money-making and property, and military offices, and public speaking, and the various offices and plots and parties that come up in the state and thinking that I was really too honourable to engage in those activities and live, refrained from those things by which I should have been of no use to you or to myself, and devoted myself to conferring upon each citizen individually what I regard as the greatest benefit? For I tried to persuade each of you to care for himself and his own perfection in goodness and wisdom rather than for any of his belongings, and for the state itself rather than for its interests, and to follow the same method in his care for other things. What, then, does such a man as I deserve? Some good thing, men of Athens, if I must propose something truly in accordance with my deserts; and the good thing should be such as is fitting for me.

Now what is fitting for a poor man who is your benefactor, and who needs leisure to exhort you? There is nothing, men of Athens, so fitting as that such a man be given his meals in the Prytaneum. That is much more appropriate for me than for any of you who has won a race at the Olympic games with a pair of horses. For he makes you seem to be happy, whereas I make you happy in reality; and he is not at all in need of sustenance, but I am needy. So if I must propose a penalty in accordance with my deserts, I propose maintenance in the Prytaneum (*a common space where state guests dined*).

Perhaps some of you think that in saying this, as in what I said about lamenting and imploring, I am speaking in a spirit of bravado; but that is not the case. The truth is rather that I am convinced that *I never intentionally wronged any one*; but I cannot convince you of this, for we have conversed with each other only a little while. I believe if you had a law, as some other people have, that *capital cases should not be decided in one day*, but only after several days, you would be convinced but now it is not easy to rid you of great prejudices in a short time. Since, then, I am convinced that I never wronged any one, I am certainly not going to wrong myself, and to say of myself that I deserve anything bad, and to propose any penalty of that sort for myself.

Why should I? Through fear of the penalty that Meletus proposes, about which I say that I do not know whether it is a good thing or an evil? Shall I choose instead of that something which I know to be an evil? What penalty shall I propose? Imprisonment?

And why should I live in prison a slave to those who may be in authority? Or shall I propose a fine, with imprisonment until it is paid? But that is the same as what I said just now, for I have no money to pay with. Shall I then propose exile as my penalty?

Perhaps you would accept that. I must indeed be possessed by a great love of life if I am so irrational as not to know that if you, who are my fellow citizens, could not endure my conversation and my words, but found them too irksome and disagreeable, so that you are now seeking to be rid of them, others will not be willing to endure them. No, men of Athens, they certainly will not. A fine life I should lead if I went away at my time of life, wandering from city to city and always being driven out! For well I know that wherever I go, the young men will listen to my talk, as they do here; and if I drive them away, they will themselves persuade their elders to drive me out, and if I do not drive them away, their fathers and relatives will drive me out for their sakes.

Perhaps someone might say: Socrates, can you not go away from us and live quietly, without talking? Now this is the hardest thing to make some of you believe. For if *I say that such conduct would be disobedience to the god* and that therefore I cannot keep quiet, you will think I am jesting and will not believe me; and if again I say that to talk every day about virtue and the other things about which you hear me talking and examining myself and others is the greatest good to man, and *that the unexamined life is not worth living*, you will believe me still less. This is as I say, gentlemen, but it is not easy to convince you. Besides, I am not accustomed to think that I deserve anything bad. If I had money, I would have proposed a fine, as large as I could pay; for that would have done me no harm.

But as it is I have no money, unless you are willing to impose a fine which I could pay. I might perhaps pay a mina of silver.

...It is no long time, men of Athens, which you gain, and for that those who wish to cast a slur upon the state will give you the name and blame of having killed Socrates, a wise man; For, you know, those who wish to revile you will say I am wise, even though I am not. Now if you had waited a little while, what you desire would have come to you of its own accord; for you see how old I am, how far advanced in life and how near death. I say this not to all of you, but to those who voted for my death.

And to them also I have something else to say. Perhaps you think, gentlemen, that I have been convicted through lack of such words as would have moved you to acquit me, if I had thought it right to do and say everything to gain an acquittal. Far from it.

And yet it is through a lack that I have been convicted, not however a lack of words, but of impudence and shamelessness, and of willingness to say to you such things as you would have liked best to hear. You would have liked to hear me wailing and lamenting and doing and saying many things which are, as I maintain, unworthy of me such things as you are accustomed to hear from others. But I did not think at the time that I ought, on account of the danger I was in, to do anything unworthy of a free man, nor do I now repent of having made my defence as I did, but I much prefer to die after such a defence than to live after a defence of the other sort. For neither in the court nor in war ought I or any other man to plan to escape death by every possible means. In battles it is often plain that a man might avoid death by throwing down his arms and begging mercy of his pursuers; and there are many other means of escaping death in dangers of various kinds if one is willing to do and say anything. But, gentlemen, it is not hard to escape death; it is much harder to escape wickedness, for that runs faster than death. And now I, *since I am slow and old, am caught by the slower runner, and my accusers, who are clever and quick, by the faster, wickedness*.

And now I shall go away convicted by you and sentenced to death, and they go convicted by truth of villainy and wrong. And I abide by my penalty, and they by theirs. Perhaps these things had to be so, and I think they are well. And now I wish to prophesy to you, O ye who have condemned me; for I am now at the time when men most do prophesy, the time just before death. And I say to you, ye men who have slain me, that punishment will come upon you straight-way after my death, far more grievous in sooth than the punishment of death which you have meted out to me. For now you have done this to me because you hoped that you would be relieved from rendering an account of your lives, but I say that you will find the result far different.

Those who will force you to give an account will be more numerous than heretofore; men whom I restrained, though you knew it not; and they will be harsher, inasmuch as they are younger, and you will be more annoyed. *For if you think that by putting men to death you will prevent anyone from reproaching you because you do not act as you should, you are mistaken*. That mode of escape is neither possible at all nor honourable, but the easiest and most honourable escape is not by suppressing others, but by making yourselves as good as possible. So with this prophecy to you who condemned me I take my leave.

But with those who voted for my acquittal I should like to converse about this which has happened, while the authorities are busy and before I go to the place where I must die. Wait with me so long, my friends; for nothing prevents our chatting with each other while there is time. I feel that you are my friends, and I wish to show you the meaning of this which has now happened to me. For, judges and in calling you judges I give you your right name a wonderful thing has happened to me. For *hitherto the customary prophetic monitor always spoke to me very frequently and opposed me even in very small matters, if I was going to do anything I should no*t; but now, as you yourselves see, this thing which might be thought, and is generally considered, the greatest of evils has come upon me; *but the divine sign did not oppose me* either when I left my home in the morning, or when I came here to the court, or at any point of my speech, when I was going to say anything; and yet on other occasions it stopped me at many points in the midst of a speech; but now, in this affair, it has not opposed me in anything I was doing or saying. What then do I suppose is the reason?

I will tell you. This which has happened to me is doubtless a good thing, and those of us who think death is an evil must be mistaken. A convincing proof of this has been given me; for the accustomed sign would surely have opposed me if I had not been going to meet with something good.

Let us consider in another way also how good reason there is to hope that it is a good thing. For the state of death is one of two things: either it is virtually nothingness, so that the dead have no consciousness of anything, or it is, as people say, a change and migration of the soul from this to another place. And if it is unconsciousness, like a sleep in which the sleeper does not even dream, death would be a wonderful gain. For I think if any one were to pick out that night in which he slept a dreamless sleep and, comparing with it the other nights and days of his life, were to say, after due consideration, how many days and nights in his life had passed more pleasantly than that night, I believe that not only any private person, but even the great King of Persia himself would find that they were few in comparison with the other days and nights.

So if such is the nature of death, I count it a gain; for in that case, all time seems to be no longer than one night. But on the other hand, if death is, as it were, a change of habitation from here to some other place, and if what we are told is true, that all the dead are there, what greater blessing could there be, judges? For if a man when he reaches the other world, after leaving behind these who claim to be judges, shall find those who are really judges who are said to sit in judgment there...who were just men in their lives, would the change of habitation be undesirable? I think that would not be unpleasant. And the greatest pleasure would be to pass my time in examining and investigating the people there, as I do those here, to find out who among them is wise and who thinks he is when he is not.

But you also, judges, must regard death hopefully and *must bear in mind this one truth, that no evil can come to a good man either in life or after death, and God does not neglect him*. So, too, this which has come to me has not come by chance, but I see plainly that it was better for me to die now and be freed from troubles. That is the reason why the sign never interfered with me, and I am not at all angry with those who condemned me or with my accusers. And yet it was not with that in view that they condemned and accused me, but because they thought to injure me. They deserve blame for that…

But now the time has come to go away. I go to die, and you to live; but which of us goes to the better lot, is known to none but God. (Plato, *Apology*, 36e–ff.)

## The Final Hours

*Plato recreates the last hours of Socrates's life in the* Phaedo. *The dialogue opens with a recall of the day that Socrates was to die. The conversation takes place some time after the execution of Socrates, though dramatically it is set on the day of his death, somewhere between June and July 399* BCE. *The major theme of the dialogue is immortality of the soul; a Pythagorean-Platonic doctrine. Standard Greek ideas of the afterlife did not conceive the soul as immortal.*

*Echecrates*: Were you with Socrates yourself, Phaedo, on the day when he drank the poison in prison, or did you hear about it from someone else?

*Phaedo*: I was there myself, Echecrates.

*Ech*: Then what did he say before his death, and how did he die? What took place at his death, Phaedo?

What was said and done? And which of his friends were with him?

*Phaedo*: For my part, I had strange emotions when I was there. For I was not filled with pity as I might naturally be when present at the death of a friend; since he seemed to me to be happy, both in his bearing and his words, he was meeting death so fearlessly and nobly. And so I thought that even in going to the abode of the dead he was not going without the protection of the gods, and that when he arrived there it would be well with him, if it ever was well with anyone. And for this reason I was not at all filled with pity, as might seem natural when I was present at a scene of mourning; nor on the other hand did I feel pleasure because we were occupied with philosophy, as was our custom and our talk was of philosophy; but a very strange feeling came over me, an unaccustomed mixture of pleasure and of pain together, when I thought that Socrates was presently to die. And all of us who were there were in much the same condition, sometimes laughing and sometimes weeping; especially one of us, Apollodorus; you know him and his character... He was quite unrestrained, and I was much agitated myself, as were the others.

*Ech*: Who were these, Phaedo?

*Phaedo*: Of native Athenians there was this Apollodorus, and Critobulus and his father, and Hermogenes and Epiganes and Aeschines and Antisthenes; and Ctesippus... and Menexenus and some other Athenians. But Plato, I think, was ill.

*Ech*: Were any foreigners there?

*Phaedo*: Yes, Simmias of Thebes and Cebes and Phaedonides, and from Megara Euclides and Terpsion.

...

*Phaedo*: In the evening we heard that the ship had arrived from Delos. So we agreed to come to the usual place as early in the morning as possible. And we came, and the jailer who usually answered the door came out and told us to wait and not go in until he told us. For, he said, the Eleven are releasing Socrates from his fetters and giving directions how he is to die today. So after a little delay he came and told us to go in. We went in then and found Socrates just released from his fetters and Xanthippe you know her with his little son in her arms, sitting beside him. Now when Xanthippe saw us, she cried out and said the kind of thing that women always do say:

Oh Socrates, this is the last time now that your friends will speak to you or you to them. And Socrates glanced at Crito and said: Crito, let somebody take her home.

And some of Crito's people took her away wailing and beating her breast. But Socrates sat up on his couch and bent his leg and rubbed it with his hand, and while he was rubbing it, he said,

— What a strange thing, my friends, that seems to be which men call pleasure! How wonderfully it is related to that which seems to be its opposite, pain, in that they will not both come to a man at the same time, and yet if he pursues the one and captures it, he is generally obliged to take the other also, as if the two were joined together in one head. And I think if

Aesop had thought of them, he would have made a fable telling how they were at war and god wished to reconcile them, and when he could not do that, he fastened their heads together, and for that reason, when one of them comes to anyone, the other follows after. Just so it seems that in my case, after pain was in my leg on account of the fetter, pleasure appears to have come following after.

Here Cebes interrupted and said, By Zeus, Socrates, I am glad you reminded me.

Several others have asked about the poems you have composed, the metrical versions of Aesop's fables and the hymn to Apollo, and Evenus asked me the day before yesterday why you, who never wrote any poetry before, composed these verses after you came to prison. Now, if you care that I should be able to answer Evenus when he asks me again and I know he will ask me, tell me what to say.

*—Then tell him, Cebes, said he, the truth, that I composed these… because I wished to test the meaning of certain dreams, and to make sure that I was neglecting no duty in case their repeated commands meant that I must cultivate the Muses in this way. They were something like this. The same dream came to me often in my past life, sometimes in one form and some-times in another, but always saying the same thing: 'Socrates,' it said, 'make music and work at it.' And I formerly thought it was urging and encouraging me to do what I was doing already and that just as people*

*encourage runners by cheering, so the dream was encouraging me to do what I was doing, that is, to make music, because philosophy was the greatest kind of music and I was working at that. But now, after the trial and while the festival of the god delayed my execution, I thought, in case the repeated dream really meant to tell me to make this which is ordinarily called music, I ought to do so and not to disobey. For I thought it was safer not to go hence before making sure that I had done what I ought, by obeying the dream and composing verses.*

*...So tell Evenus that and bid him farewell, and tell him, if he is wise, to come after me as quickly as he can. It seems, I am going to-day; for that is the order of the Athenians. (Plato,* Phaedo, *57a–61c.)*

## His Last Words

*After a long discussion of the nature and immortality of the soul (a Platonic-Pythagorean idea), the dialogue ends with Socrates*'s *final moments and his last words. Having recounted a myth of the afterlife, Socrates says,*

You, Simmias and Cebes and the rest, he said, will go hereafter, each in his own time; but I am now already, as a tragedian would say, called by fate, and it is about time for me to go to the bath; for I think it is better to bathe before drinking the poison, that the women may not have the trouble of bathing the corpse.

When he had finished speaking, Crito said: Well, Socrates, do you wish to leave any directions with us about your children or anything else anything we can do to serve you?

— What I always say, Crito, if you take care of yourselves you will serve me and mine and yourselves, whatever you do, even if you make no promises now; but if you neglect yourselves and are not willing to live following step by step, as it were, in the path marked out by our present and past discussions, you will accomplish nothing, no matter how much or how eagerly you promise at present.

...

But how shall we bury you?

— However you please, he replied, if you can catch me and I do not get away from you. And he laughed gently, and looking towards us, said: I cannot persuade Crito, my friends, that the Socrates who is now conversing and arranging the details of his argument is really I; he thinks I am the one whom he will presently see as a corpse, and he asks how to bury me. And though I have been saying at great length that after I drink the poison I shall no longer be with you, but shall go away to the joys of the blessed you know of, he seems to think that was idle talk uttered to encourage you and myself... Dear Crito... You must be of good courage, and say that you bury my body, and bury it as you think best and as seems to you most fitting.

When he had said this, he got up and went into another room to bathe; Crito followed him, but he told us to wait... And when he had bathed and his children had been brought to him for he had two little sons and one big one and the women of the family had come, he talked with them in Crito's presence and gave them such directions as he wished; then he told the women to go away, and he came to us. And it was now nearly sunset; for he had spent a long time within. And he came and sat down fresh from the bath. After that not much was said, and the servant of the Eleven (*the 'corrections officers' who supervised prisons*) came and stood beside him and said:

— Socrates, I shall not find fault with you, as I do with others, for being angry and cursing me, when at the behest of the authorities, I tell them to drink the poison. No, I have found you in all this time in every way the noblest and gentlest and best man who has ever come here, and now I know your anger is directed against others, not against me, for you know who are to blame. Now, for you know the message I came to bring you, farewell and try to bear what you must as easily as you can. And he burst into tears and turned and went away.

And Socrates looked up at him and said: Fare you well, I too will do as you say;

And then he said to us: How charming the man is! Ever since I have been here he has been coming to see me and talking with me from time to time, and has been the best of men, and now how nobly he weeps for me! But come, Crito, let us obey him, and let someone bring the poison, if it is ready; and if not, let the man prepare it.

And Crito said: But I think, Socrates, the sun is still upon the mountains and has not yet set; I know that others have taken the poison very late, after the order has come to them, and in the meantime have eaten and drunk and some of them enjoyed the society of those whom they loved. Do not hurry; for there is still time.

And Socrates said: Crito, those whom you mention are right in doing as they do, for they think they gain by it; and I shall be right in not doing as they do; for I think I should gain nothing by taking the poison a little later. I should only make myself ridiculous in my own eyes if I clung to life when there is no more profit in it.

Come, he said, do as I ask and do not refuse.

Thereupon Crito nodded to the boy who was standing near. The boy went out then came back with the man who was to administer the poison, which he brought with him in a cup ready for use. And when Socrates saw him, he said:

— Well, my good man, you know about these things; what must I do?

— Nothing, he replied, except drink the poison and walk about till your legs feel heavy; then lie down, and the poison will take effect of itself.

At the same time he held out the cup to Socrates. He took it, and very gently, Echecrates, without trembling or changing colour or expression, but looking up at the man with wide open eyes, as was his custom, said: What do you say about pouring a libation to some deity from this cup? May I, or not?

— Socrates, said he, we prepare only as much as we think is enough.

> *— I understand said Socrates; but I may and must pray to the gods that my departure hence be a fortunate one; and so I offer this prayer, and may it be granted.*

With these words he raised the cup to his lips and very cheerfully and quietly drained it. Up to that time most of us had been able to restrain our tears fairly well, but when we watched him drinking and saw that he had drunk the poison, we could do so no longer, but in spite of myself my tears rolled down in floods, so that I wrapped my face in my cloak and wept for myself; for it was not for him that I wept, but for my own misfortune in being deprived of such a friend. Crito had got up and gone away even before I did, because he could not restrain his tears. But Apollodorus, who had been weeping all the time before, then wailed aloud in his grief and made us all break down, except Socrates himself. But he said: What conduct is this, you strange men! I sent the women away chiefly for this very reason, that they might not behave in this absurd way; for I have heard that it is best to die in silence. Keep quiet and be brave.

Then we were ashamed and controlled our tears. He walked about and, when he said his legs were heavy, lay down on his back, for such was the advice of the attendant.

The man who had administered the poison laid his hands on him and after a while examined his feet and legs, then pinched his foot hard and asked if he felt it. He said

No; then after that, his thighs; and passing upwards in this way he showed us that he was growing cold and rigid. And again he touched him and said that when it reached his heart, he would be gone. The chill had now reached the region about the groin, and uncovering his face, which had been covered, he said and these were his last words.

*Crito*: we owe a cock to Asclepius. Pay it and do not neglect it.

That, said Crito, shall be done; but see if you have anything else to say. To this question he made no reply, but after a little while he moved; the attendant uncovered him; his eyes were fixed. And Crito, when he saw it, closed his mouth and eyes.

Such was the end, Echecrates, of our friend, who was, as we may say, of all those of his time whom we have known, the best and wisest and most righteous man.

*The sacrifice to Asclepius, Socrates's last words according to Plato, has been the subject of much discussion. Asclepius was the god of health (and so of medicine). It was customary to make such a sacrifice on being cured of some disease. The major theme of the dialogue was to provide a proof of the immortality of the soul (a radical doctrine which Socrates may not have held). Here, through his last words, Plato says that Socrates was finally freed of his body, his death the cure for his mortality.*

# GLOSSARY

All dates unless specified are Before Common Era (BCE).

**Antisthenes:** Student of Gorgias and Socrates; teacher, writer of Socratic dialogues. Xenophon describes him as Socrates's constant companion. Only fragments of his writings remain.

**Anytus, Lycon, Meletus:** Socrates's accusers. In 399 BCE Anytus, whose son was executed by the Thirty, joined Meletus's prosecution. Meletus was the primary plaintiff. In the *Apology* Socrates says, 'if Anytus and Lycon had not joined him, he would have been fined a thousand *drachmae* for not receiving a fifth of the votes.'

**Alcibiades:** Descended on both sides from families that were among Athens's first and most powerful, he was an acolyte of Socrates. Two Platonic dialogues are named after him. In Plato's *Symposium* he praises Socrates. A major player in Athenian politics of the period, he eventually fled Athens to join, first the Spartans, then the Persians.

**Aeschines:** Close to Socrates; present both for his trial and the day of his execution. Fragments of two of his dialogues, the *Alcibiades* and *Aspasia* remain.

**Amphipolis:** City in Northern Greece where in the 10th Year of the Peloponnesian war (422 BCE), the Spartans defeated the Athenians. Cleon, the elected leader of the Athenians was killed there, as was the Spartan general, Brasidas.

**Apollodorus:** Nicknamed 'maniac'. Xenophon describes him and Antisthenes as two men who never left Socrates's side. He was present at Socrates's trial and offered money for his fine. He was the most emotional of those gathered at Socrates's execution.

**Archelaus:** Tyrant of Macedonia, son of Perdiccas II, allied with Athens, patronized the poet Agathon (Plato's *Symposium* is set at his house). Admired by Callicles in Plato's *Gorgias*.

**Arginusae:** In 406 BCE six generals, accused of failing to rescue the wounded and dead after the sea battle at Arginusae were sentenced to death. They were tried as a group, in violation of Athenian law. Socrates attempted, but failed to prevent their execution.

**Aristophanes:** Comic Playwright. Eleven of his plays survive. Made fun of Socrates in the *Clouds*. Plato's treatment of Aristophanes in the *Symposium* is sympathetic. Only Aristophanes and Agathon are able to stay awake all night with Socrates. An epitaph for him is attributed to Plato: 'The Graces, seeking for themselves a shrine that would not fall, found the soul of Aristophanes.'

**Aspasia:** Aspasia lived as the *de facto* wife of Pericles. for about twenty years from 450 BCE until his death in 429 BCE. In Plato's *Menexenus,* Socrates identifies Aspasia as his, and Pericles's instructor in oratory. Cicero reports that Athenians annually recited Plato's *Funeral Speech* along with Pericles's speech in honor of the war dead.

**Callias:** One of the richest men in Greece. An example of Plato putting well-known living persons into the dialogues. The comic poets followed the trail of Callias's money and scandal: Aristophanes represented him in *Birds* as a hoopoe plucked nearly featherless by females and malicious plaintiffs.

**Cebes:** Discusses immortality of the soul with Socrates in the Phaedo. Cebes was alive in 354 BCE when *Letter* 7 was written. Xenophon says only that he was a member of Socrates's inner circle.

**Chaerephon:** A younger contemporary of Socrates, who says they have been friends since their youth. Plato depicts him as a little mad. It was Chaerephon who consulted the oracle at Delphi and was told that no one was wiser than Socrates. He was a favourite of the comic poets for two decades.

**Charmides:** In the *Protagoras*, he appears with the sons of Pericles in the group flanking Protagoras. Though not one of the Thirty, he was sympathetic to their cause, and was killed in the battle that restored the democracy.

**Callicles:** A member of the aristocracy. In the *Gorgias* Callicles favours the 'tyrannical man', both the product and the deadliest enemy of democracy. Plato's representation of Callicles in the *Gorgias* appealed to Nietzsche.

**Cleon:** Pro-war democratic leader. Pilloried by Aristophanes.

**Critias:** In Plato's *Timaeus*, Critias tells the company that he was about ten years old when his ninety-year-old grandfather told him Solon's Atlantis story. To be distinguished from the Critias who was leader of the oligarchy of the Thirty, and was killed in battle with the returning democratic forces.

**Crito:** Xenophon counts Crito among Socrates's inner circle. In Plato's *Apology* he offers funds for Socrates's fine. In the *Crito* he arranges for Socrates to escape from prison. The conversation on Law follows on Socrates's refusal to escape.

**Critobulus:** Son of Crito. Critobulus can be placed within the inner circle of Socrates's associates because of his presence at both the trial and death of Socrates. He was one of those who also offered money for Socrates's fine.

**Delium**: Battle fought in the eighth year of the Peloponnesian war. After a long struggle, the Athenians retreated, pursued by the Boeotian cavalry. It is Socrates's heroic behavior during the retreat that Laches and Alcibiades commend.

**Delphi:** The ruins of the Temple of Apollo, visible today, date from the fourth century BCE. These include a number of statues, and numerous 'treasuries'. built by several Greek city-states to thank the oracle for her advice. The most impressive is the-restored Athenian Treasury, built to commemorate their victory at the Battle of Marathon in 490 BCE.

**Diogenes Laërtius (flourished third century CE):** Greek author noted for his history of Greek Philosophy, the most important secondary source for this period.

**Diotima:** The wise woman whose discourse on Love Socrates reports in Plato's *Symposium*, There is general agreement that Diotima is the *one* named character that Plato invented.

**Eucleides:** According to Diogenes, Plato and other Socratics visited Euclides in Megara after the death of Socrates. Socratic dialogues attributed to Euclides include *Lamprias, Crito. Eroticus*, *Alcibiades*; none survive.

**Euthydemus:** Beloved of Critias, would-be beloved of Socrates.

**Euthyphro:** In Plato's *Euthyphro* he is a prophet who has brought a charge of homicide against his father. Ironically, he offers to instruct Socrates on the nature of piety.

**Gorgias:** Of Leontini (eastern Sicily), renowned rhetorician. His visit to Athens as an ambassador in 427 BCE had a far-reaching impact on the practice of rhetoric in Athens. Gorgias lived at least 105 years.

**Hermogenes:** Appears in several Platonic dialogues. He was present at Socrates's death. Hermogenes is Xenophon's chief source for Socrates's trial and execution when Xenophon was campaigning in Persia.

**Hippias of Elis:** Polymath, sophist, mathematician, diplomat. At least one of two Platonic dialogues named after him is genuine. Socrates discuses justice and law with him in Xenophon's Memorablia.

**Laches:** Laches was elected general in 427/6 BCE and commanded the fleet in Sicily, Laches was with Socrates on the retreat from Delium in 424 BCE. Alcibiades said. that Socrates saved them both by swaggering so fiercely that enemy soldiers did not dare to approach them.

**Menexenus:** Of Athens, among those present at Socrates's death. Plato names a dialogue after him

**Meno:** Student of Gorgias. Plato in his dialogue of that name, represents Meno as wealthy and under the influence of Gorgias.

**Peloponnesian War (431–404 BCE):** War fought between Athens and Sparta the two leading cities in ancient Greece. Their allies included nearly every Greek city-state, engulfing the whole of Greece in the 27 year war. Thucydides wrote a detailed account of its progress.

**Plato:** Plato came of age towards the end of the Peloponnesian war in 405 BCE. In 399 BCE, the year of Socrates's execution, he was well on his way to a political career.

**Phaedo:** Student of Socrates, founded a school of philosophy at Elis. Main speaker in the dialogue, named after him.

**Polemarchus:** Belonged to a very wealthy merchant family. During the rule of the Thirty, Polemarchus was forced to drink hemlock. With all the family's goods seized, neighbours contributed a cloak for his shroud. In the *Republic*, set well before these events, Polemarchus held that one should help friends and harm enemies.

**Polus of Acragas (Sicily):** Student of Gorgias the rhetorician. His name means 'colt'. Polus is credited with the invention of rhetorical terms.

**Polycrates**: Rhetorician, author of *The Indictment of Socrate*s, said to be the speech Anytus delivered at Socrates's trial but was not, in fact, written until later.

**Plutarch:** Greek philosopher, historian, biographer, and priest at the Temple of Apollo in Delphi. Among his approximately 227 works are the *Parallel Lives*, (biographies of illustrious Greeks and Romans), and the *Moralia*, on ethical religious, political, and literary topics.

**Potidaea:** Battle fought in 432 BCE. During the retreat, Socrates saved a wounded Alcibiades. What was left of the army reached a plague ridden Athens only in May of 429 BCE, having been away nearly three years.

**Protagoras of Abdera:** Renowned sophist who lived in Athens for many years. Protagoras wrote a work called *Truth*, and probably much more. His 'masterful' speech in defence of the Athenian democracy, in the dialogue named after him, was written by Plato.

**Simmias:** Pythagorean friend of Socrates. Xenophon puts him in the circle of friends closest to Socrates.He came from Thebes with money to aid in Socrates's prison escape. He was present at Socrates's death.

**Theaetetus:** Mathematician and geometer. Plato wrote the *Theaetetus* as a memorial to him when he was mortally wounded in battle in 391 BCE.

**Thirty Tyrants:** Although voted into power in 404 BCE, these oligarchs had a brief and bloody rule of eight months, putting to death 1,500 citizens without a trial, and forcing more than 5,000 to flee. Socrates refused to do their bidding.

**Thrasymachus of Chalcedon:** Thrasymachus was a rhetorician of some note, for there are numerous references to elements of his style. There is a memorable representation of him in Plato's *Republic*.

**Thucydides**: Author of the *The Peloponnesian War*. Himself a general, he arrived too late to save Amphipolis. Exiled by the Athenians for 20 years, he spent his time writing the history of that war.

**Xanthippe:** Wife of Socrates. She was probably not beyond 40 when Socrates was 70.They had three children.

**Xenophon:** An associate of Socrates. Although he writes critically of the Thirty, He is said to have remained in the city during their rule and to have fought for the oligarchy in the battle at Munychia in 403 BCE. He recorded, in his *Anabasis*, the retreat of 10,000 Greek mercenaries back through Asia to Byzantium.

# TIMELINE: IMPORTANT DATES (BCE) IN THE LIFE OF SOCRATES

| | |
|---|---|
| 469 | Birth of Socrates |
| 431 | Pelonnesian war between Athens and Sparta begins. |
| 432–430 | Battle of Potidaea Socrates fights as a hoplite (heavily armed foot soldier) |
| 429 | Socrates returns to Athens |
| 428/7 | Birth of Plato |
| 424 | Battle of Delium |
| 423 | Socrates is ridiculed in two of the three plays of the year's festival. *The Clouds* of Aristophanes wins third prize |
| 422 | Socrates fights at Amphipolis |
| 414 | Aristophanes in the Birds coins the verb 'to Socratise' |
| 406 | October, Socrates is president of Council after the sea battle at Arginusae. The trial of the generals |
| 405 | Ridiculed in Aristophanes's *Frogs* |

| | |
|---|---|
| 404 | Athens defeated by Sparta; Peloponnesian War ends Thirty Tyrants rule |
| 403 | Democracy restored |
| 399 | Trial and execution of Socrates |

***Dramatic Dates of Plato's Socratic Dialogues***

| | |
|---|---|
| *Euthyphro* | Spring 399 |
| *Apology* | May–June 399 |
| *Crito* | June–July 399 (28 days after the trial) |
| *Phaedo* | One or two days later |
| Death of Plato | 348/7 |

# A VERY SHORT BIBLIOGRAPHY

A short bibliography of writings on Socrates post 399 BCE would be much longer than this book. The titles listed here are only some of the more prominent works in English about this enigmatic figure.

Ahbel-Rappe, S. and Kamtekar R., (eds.), 2007, *A Companion to Socrates,* Blackwell.

Boys-Stones, George and Rowe, Christopher, 2013, (Ed and Trans), *The Circle of Socrates: Readings in the First-Generation Socratics*, Hackett, Indianapolis.

Brickhouse, Thomas C., and Nicholas D. Smith, 1994, *Plato's Socrates*. Clarendon Press, Oxford.

— 2002, *The Trial and Execution of Socrates*. New York, NY.

Burnyeat, M.F., 2012, *Explorations in Ancient and Modern Philosophy*. 2 vols, Cambridge.

Chroust, A.H., 1957, *Socrates, Man and Myth*. London.

Diogenes, Laertius. *Lives of Eminent Philosophers*. Vol.1, 1925, Trans. R.D. Hicks. H.U.P., Cambridge.

Dodds, E.R., 1951, *The Greeks and the Irrational*. California Univ. Press.

Field, G.C., 1967, *Plato and his Contemporaries,* Menthuen

Guthrie, W.K.C., 1969, *A History of Greek Philosophy. Vol. III*. Cambridge.

Jowett, B., 1953, *The Dialogues of Plato*, translated into English with Analyses and Introductions, 4th ed., 4 vols., Oxford.

Kahn, C.H., 1998, *Plato and the Socratic Dialogue*, Cambridge.

Kraut, Richard, 1983, *Socrates and the State*. Princeton.

McPherran, Mark L., 1996, *The Religion of Socrates,* Pennsylvania.

Nails, Debra, 2002, *The People Of Plato*, Hackett.

O'Brien, M.J., 1967, *The Socratic Paradoxes and the Greek Mind*, Chapel Hill.

Plato, *Works*, 12 vols, various dates, H.U.P. ,Cambridge.

Santas, Gerasimos X., 1979, *Socrates: Philosophy in Plato's Early Dialogues*, London.

Taylor, A.E., 1911, *Varia Socratica*. Oxford.

Vlastos, Gregory, ed. 1971, *The Philosophy of Socrates*. Garden City.

— 1991. *Socrates: Ironist and Moral Philosopher*, Cambridge.

— 1995 *Studies in Greek Philosophy* vol. 2, Princeton

Xenophon, *Works,* 1923, 7 Vols., Trans. Marchant. E.C., H.U.P, Cambridge.

# ACKNOWLEDGEMENTS

I would like to thank all the people who helped me in putting these readings together. First to the Publisher, Hachette India, and to Yukta Vats whose idea it was, in the first place, to introduce general readers to difficult thinkers. Having kick-started the idea she left me to my own devices. I go back in time to thank all the students who sat through my lectures on Greek philosophy and further back to my own teachers both at St. Stephen's College as well as McGill University, and to friends and colleagues at Delhi University — hard to name them all. Also, to my online class on Greek literature and philosophy born during the COVID-19 years and mothered by Lillianne and Urna, and many others with whom I read tragedy in those tragic times. More recently, the substance of this book and others in the pipeline, to my former and current students, Annie, Amrita, Alphy, Archana, Nandita, Priyanka, Ratna, Yashvi, and others. Not least to the many experts whom I never met but whose books I read and learned so much from. To all of them I dedicate this book and to those who still believe in the possibility of a just world.

Vijay Tankha
March 2026

*Dear Reader,*

We hope you enjoyed reading this book and we'd love your attention for one more page, to share with you what's going on with children and books.

The number of children reading in their leisure time and for fun is in rapid decline. Young people have a lot of competition for their time, and a worryingly high number have only a few or no books at home.

If this is not a crisis already, it soon will be.

Studies have shown that reading for fun is the **single biggest predictor of a child's future success** – more than family circumstance, parents' educational background or income. It improves academic results, mental health, wealth, communication skills and ambition.

Our business works committedly to create books that are well-researched, engaging, and enduring, but here are some ways we can all raise more readers:

- Reading to children for just 10 minutes a day makes a difference
- Don't give up if children aren't regular readers – it's not just about the number of books they have or read but about encouraging interest and engagement
- Encourage them to listen to audiobooks
- Support schools and other libraries
- Give books as gifts

Thank you for reading: there's a lot more information about how to encourage children to read on our website.

**www.raisingreaders.in**